Controversial Essays

*

by the same author

INDEPENDENT ESSAYS

John Sparrow

CONTROVERSIAL ESSAYS

FABER AND FABER

24 Russell Square

London

First published in mcmlxvi
by Faber and Faber Limited
24 Russell Square London WC 1
Printed in Great Britain by
R. MacLehose and Company Limited
The University Press Glasgow
All rights reserved

Contents

*

Acknowledgements

*

'The Housman Dilemma' and 'Judges in Israel' first appeared in *The Times Literary Supplement*; both essays on 'Regina *v.* Penguin Books Ltd.' are reprinted from *Encounter*. 'The Press, Politics, and Private Life' was published in an abridged form in *The New York Review of Books*.

'A Polish Plagiarist' is reprinted from *Oxford Slavonic Papers* with the permission of the Editors and Delegates.

Preface

*

When we say that a man is a 'controversial' figure we usually
mean that what he says or writes or does is likely to give rise to
dissension, if indeed it is not actually intended to provoke it. It
is in another, milder, sense that the essays here collected qualify
for the description: their aim is not to provoke dissension but
to put an end to it; they are 'controversial' simply because it is
to the region of controversy that they belong. And they belong
for the most part to the area in which, as it seems to me,
controversy is most usefully conducted, the area in which we
are called upon to exercise our judgement on questions of
fact. The questions arising in this area may be reduced
to the form: Is the evidence strong enough to warrant the conclusion that . . . ? Disagreement about aesthetic or ethical
values is not in this sense controversial; the merits, for instance,
of a particular book or picture may well be a matter upon which
opinions differ; but the clash of opinions on such a matter is not
controversy. Again, the question what moral judgment should
be passed upon a particular person, assuming that the relevant
facts are undisputed, is one that may well divide opinion; but
it is not really a matter for controversy in this sense, although
controversy might concern itself with the circumstances of his
life and the correct determination of his motives.

So, too, the question whether a man ought to have acted as
he did on a particular occasion is a question that may be de-
bated controversially if the 'ought' is prudential and the
answer depends upon a right assessment of circumstances and
consequences, but not if the disagreement concerns only the
moral quality of the act.

These essays, then, are controversial because in each case

they discuss the question whether a certain conclusion, or certain conclusions, can be justified by ascertainable facts; they do not try to persuade the reader of the validity of an ethical or aesthetic judgment by pressing upon him a certain point of view or a certain set of values; they try to convince him of the truth of a factual allegation by appealing to the evidence. 'Consider the circumstances', they say, in effect, 'observe their interrelation, weigh their significance: do you not now see that it *must* be so?'

Of course, if by appealing to general principles or to great examples one manages to persuade someone to exchange a lower for a higher set of values or to take a wider or a nobler view of life, or if one opens the eyes of one's readers to qualities in a work of literature or art that they have hitherto been unaware of, one will have done more good than one is likely to do if one influences their opinions simply by setting them right upon questions of fact. But to reveal to others the inadequacy of their standards or of their perceptiveness, in aesthetic or ethical matters, is the function not of the controversialist, but of the moralist or the critic.

The aim of the controversial writer is, comparatively, modest; but he may still do some good. If he convinces his readers of the truth of something that they have up till now denied or doubted, and thus leads them to renounce an ill-founded or unfounded opinion, he will have corrected error and thus made the world a tidier, a more rational, and, to that extent, a better place. The more important the topic on which the controversialist thus corrects erroneous opinion, and the more people he sets right by doing so, the more good he will have effected. Such is the object of these essays.

The last essay in the book well illustrates the distinction between a critical and a controversial piece of writing. It concerns the reputation of a poet who is one of the great names in the history of letters in Poland. In an earlier article I had shown (I think irrefutably) that a set of poems that had always passed as his were really the work of an Italian contemporary. Since these poems had been thought by critics to mark an epoch in the development of the lyric in Poland, my discovery meant that a chapter in Polish literary history had to be re-written, and it was not surprising that a patriotic attempt should have been made to vindicate the national hero at least from the charge of conscious plagiarism. My essay is a reply — I hope, courteous and conclusive — to that attempt. It passes no moral judgment on the plagiarist and no critical judgment on the disputed poems; it is submitted simply as a specimen of argument in support of truth.

The last essay but one concerns the work of a more familiar poet — A. E. Housman. It touches on a vexed question — how far should a writer's testamentary injunctions about his work be considered binding? — but it does not attempt to answer that question; still less does it pretend to pass a judgment on the quality of Housman's poetry. It is concerned simply with ascertaining, on the evidence of his manuscripts as presented in the book under review, what the poet must actually have written.

Two of the essays are about a novelist who was himself, in the popular sense of the epithet, a controversial writer — D. H. Lawrence. In the first of these I was concerned, as I explained in the second, simply to ascertain what Lawrence meant at a crucial point in his most 'controversial' novel. One had to grasp his meaning at this point (or so it seemed to me) if one was fully to understand the message that the novel as a whole was meant to convey; and one could not do full justice to the book either as a tract or as a work of art if one failed to understand that message and to appreciate the care with which Lawrence planted, throughout the story, half-hidden clues to the meaning of the crucial episode — a care that showed how deeply he must have pondered over that episode and how much importance he attached to its significance.

It was not the object of my essay to pronounce upon the literary value of the book or upon the justice of the verdict delivered at its trial, still less upon the morality of the acts that it described: I was writing neither as a moralist nor as a literary critic.

The first of these two essays, when it appeared, aroused much indignation among two groups of *bien pensants*, whom I may for convenience call the conventional Right and the intellectual Left; representatives of each attacked it in *Encounter* and elsewhere. Though both of these sets of critics used the forms of argument in their fulminations — some of them trying to show that my interpretation was wrong, others insisting that even if it was right the book was not one that ought to be suppressed — it seemed to me that both had lost their heads. The loss was more serious for the latter than for the former, and more in their case to be deplored, because it led them to compromise the cause of Reason and of Art, of which they ought to be (and claimed to be) especially the champions.

The critics of the 'Right' were blinded — as it appeared to me — by indignation at the 'immorality' of the book (all the worse, in their opinion, if my interpretation of it was correct); those of the 'Left' abandoned a rational approach in their desire to vindicate the supposed rights of the artist and to prove their own broadmindedness and progressive outlook — and also in their eagerness, at the trial itself, simply to win the day. Both sides, in consequence, failed to do justice to the issues, raised by my article, that underlay the trial. Some of these issues, indeed, concerned law and morals, and lay outside the field of controversy proper as I have defined it; my views upon these were not really relevant to the main point I had to make.

Looking back now upon the controversy, I cannot help feeling that, on every point at issue, it was I that was in the right and my critics that were in the wrong. It is now (I think) generally admitted that my interpretation of the story was correct; I see no reason to change my opinion that if that interpretation had been brought home to the jury they might well have condemned the book instead of acquitting it; and I still think that, in that event, it would have been wrong of the jury to allow themselves to be so affected by the revelation (see p. 66 *infr*.). I still believe that the need to preserve public decency affords a more plausible justification for the censor's activities than the need to protect public morals (see p. 67); I still find it difficult (see p. 67) to decide at what point the censor should be allowed to interfere, whatever grounds the case for censorship is based on; I am still of opinion that the merits of Lawrence's book, whether as a work of art or as a social tract, were greatly over-rated by most of the witnesses in the case; and I still think it a pity that Penguin Books Ltd. should have launched hundreds of thousands of cheap copies of the novel upon the world, and that a number of persons whose words, apparently, carried weight with the public should have helped to make it possible for them to do so.

One result of the case has been that, in the words of Mr. George Steiner, 'Since the Lady Chatterley case and the defeat of a number of attempts to suppress books by Henry Miller, the sluice gates stand open', and through them have poured into the bookshops a number of erotic books, published by Mr. Maurice Girodias and others, whose pretensions to literary merit are considered by Mr. Steiner in the article from which I have quoted.[1] It can hardly be denied that such books, like all fiction and imaginative writing, in prose or verse, may affect, for better or worse, the minds and behaviour of those who read them. Indeed, I should have supposed this to be too obvious to need assertion, were it not frequently challenged in attacks upon censorship even by critics who, paradoxically, deplore cruel books and films as being likely to brutalize the young. 'It is a gross over-simplification' — so runs the argument — 'to allege a causal relationship between a book or film and the subsequent behaviour of any person who reads the one or sees the other; it is impossible to prove that anyone has ever behaved worse for having seen or read an "indecent" film or book'. I

[1] 'Night Words: High Pornography and Human Privacy', in *Encounter*, October, 1965.

should rather have said that some books inspire their readers to good actions while others cause them (if I may use simple language) to do bad things that they would not otherwise have done. To take an extreme example in the field of sex: the works of the Marquis de Sade (which seem to me to be devoid of literary merit, whatever Swinburne and Mr. Girodias may say about them), while they might reinforce by repulsion the 'virtue' of some readers, might impel a young person with strong sexual instincts — given a cool head and favourable circumstances — to commit a series of cold-blooded murders. Even so mild a book as *Lady Chatterley* — much more, the sort of pornography purveyed by Mr. Girodias and his rivals — might, however lofty the intentions of the publisher, encourage the inexperienced to indulge their sexual appetites with little or no discrimination or restraint. Whether this is a bad thing, and if so how bad it is, and how far it is possible or desirable to prevent it by censorship or by other means — these are questions that I do not claim to answer; I only suggest that erotic books, like books of any other kind, may directly inspire action on the part of those who read them.

People who approve of the dissemination of pornographic books would claim, no doubt, that even if they shock some people and have a deleterious effect upon the behaviour of others, the price is well worth paying in view of the freedom that the decision in the Chatterley case effectively procured both for the writer and for his readers.

This claim rests on an assumption about 'freedom' that seems to me to be the opposite of the truth. Whatever may be the direct influence of books of this kind, their dissemination produces an indirect effect subtler, more diffusive, and more deplorable both on literature and on society at large. So far from deepening or extending the range of possible human emotion, in literature or in life, books that describe the physical side of love without reticence and in detail, like people who encourage us all to abandon conventional inhibitions about sex in language and public behaviour, tend to restrict the very freedom they intend to protect and to enlarge. For all their 'realism', such books, like manuals of sex, must fall as far short of conveying the actuality of passion as the horticulturalist's catalogue falls short of conveying the actuality of the flowers that it meticulously describes. The poets and novelists who have been most successful in conveying the passion of love have succeeded as much by what they left unsaid as by what they actually expressed; and this reticence is not due to prudency or cowardice; it is, it seems, almost a necessary condition of the writer's art when it deals with that realm of experience.

It would be easy to produce examples suggesting that this is so; to say why it should be so is not so easy. I am not tempted to use the word 'sacred' though it is a favourite in this context with both Lawrence's admirers and his critics; I would rather put it that there is an element of mystery in passionate love, and that writers who think that justice can be done to that complex experience by relentless insistence on physical particulars, so far from enlarging their own or their readers' consciousness, restrict its range and impoverish its quality.

Lawrence himself affords an example of the truth of this. When he wrote about love, he wrote like a poet; he could not have written like a pornographer if he had tried; but the doctrinaire of sex was at war in him with the poet of love, and it was when he tried hardest, as in *Lady Chatterley*, to be full and frank and fearless in his description of sexual experience that he failed most signally to convey the reality of passion.

If imaginative literature is impoverished by those writers who believe that full justice cannot be done to passionate experience except by describing it in terms of sex, life itself is equally degraded and vulgarized by those who insist that there should be no shame or secrecy about sexual behaviour, and that 'sex' is just another natural function, like eating and drinking, with no mystery about it and no stronger claim to privacy than the other activities that make up human life.

Preface

The second essay in this book also deals with privacy and convention, in a more specialized context. What are the limits on the right conferred on the individual by the conventions of civilized Western society to insist on the privacy of his private life? Of all the questions agitated in the affair of Stephen Ward and the Minister for War, that seemed to me the most interesting and the most important. The line that I adopted in discussing it exposed me, again, to criticism from both the conventional Right and the intellectual Left, and a respectable London periodical refused to print my essay. Journalists, thirsting for salacious 'copy' and smarting from the humiliation of their exposure in the Vassall case, and politicians, eager to 'smear' the Government or to undermine it, joined in branding as 'hypocritical' the position that I defended. It still seems to me that there was more hypocrisy in the appeals made by the other side to 'security risks' and 'Augean stables'.

Now that the smoke has cleared away from the field of battle between the censor and Penguin Books, and now that the mud slung at the authorities by Lord Kennet and Mr. Ludovic Kennedy has had time to dry, I hope that the arguments and assessments offered in these essays will afford an acceptable basis for a judgment by their readers. To pass moral judgments is not, I have suggested, the proper business of the controversialist; but, as the case of Eichmann dealt with in the first essay may remind us, it is the inescapable responsibility of all those who think and feel.

Controversial Essays

*

Judges in Israel
The Case of Adolf Eichmann

*

'Christ says "judge not"; *but we must judge*', so Dean Inge; and surely the Decanal is to be preferred to the Divine injunction. Those who refuse ever to pass sentence on their fellow-men may be actuated by the noblest of motives, but they fail in their duty as members of a society acknowledging the authority of a moral law. If, in this workaday world, we wait for the sinless to cast the first stone, crime will remain long unpunished and wickedness go for ever unreproved.

Perhaps, however, the Gospel exhortation should be taken not as a guide to action but as a warning to those who are too ready to condemn the erring, a plea for deeper understanding of impugned behaviour: if you really understand, it may even imply, the grounds for condemnation will disappear: *tout comprendre, c'est tout pardonner*. But then, ought we to try to understand Hitler completely, if complete understanding will lead us to tolerate or condone his actions? (Indeed, the maxim really requires us to tolerate them even if our understanding is imperfect, for it would be wrong that another should suffer for a failure in our own percipience.) And why, after all, we may ask, should understanding necessitate forgiveness? Forgiveness implies a recognition that guilt exists — and a readiness to overlook it that springs not from the intelligence but from the heart. If the understanding is to play any part in the process, it must surely be at an earlier stage, by removing the concept of guilt itself; full insight might reveal in human behaviour an ineluctable process of cause and effect that negates the possibility of moral differentiation between one action and another:

3

tout comprendre, c'est rien pardonner — for him who really understands, perhaps, there is nothing to forgive.

Those who believe in the existence of moral values will not be
able to accept this solution. So long as there are duties, they
will insist, we have a duty to judge — and to judge, so far as in
us lies, correctly; but we may be helped to right judgment —
and Christ's words may serve to remind us of the fact — by
humility and by that product of intelligence and sympathy that
is called imagination.

Mr. Moshe Pearlman, in his approach to Eichmann's trial,[1]
does not seem to be much troubled by imagination, by humility,
or by awareness of the finer issues involved in the act of moral
judgment. His solid volume of more than 600 pages, which
recounts Eichmann's story from the moment when the kid-
nappers pounced on their prey in an obscure suburb of Buenos
Aires to the dawn hour two years later when his ashes were
scattered over the Mediterranean, reads from beginning to end
like nothing so much as a piece of propaganda from the pen of
an unofficial Public Relations Officer of the State of Israel. He
is assailed by no doubts about the juridical validity of the
proceedings or the ethical foundations upon which they were
based; he describes with unattractive relish the hunting-down
and capture of the fugitive; he records with apparent satisfaction the 'roar of applause' that broke out in the Knesset when
the Prime Minister announced that Eichmann was to be
brought to trial; he regards the prisoner quite simply as 'the
man who personified the forces of darkness'; and he exhibits
his captive in the glass dock in the Jerusalem court-room as if
he were a noxious insect in a killing-bottle, spinning and
twitching convulsively, in full view of a gratified audience, who
know as well as does their victim that he is doomed.

Mr. Pearlman's book at least performs one service for the

[1] Moshe Pearlman: *The Capture and Trial of Adolf Eichmann.* 666 pp.
Weidenfeld and Nicolson.

student who is interested in the 'literature' concerning Eichmann's trial: it makes it easier to understand, if not to accept, the spirit in which Dr. Hannah Arendt composed her study of the proceedings.[1] *Eichmann in Jerusalem* grew out of the 'eye-witness' account of the trial that its author wrote for the *New Yorker*, but its primary purpose would seem to be to protest against just such propaganda as is served up by Mr. Pearlman.

Dr. Arendt is well aware of the diffidence that should attend a moral judgment on any issue, and in particular on the issues underlying the case before her; she does not indeed defend Eichmann, but she is measured in her condemnation of him; she does not see him as the personification of 'the forces of darkness' or, in the prosecution's phrase, 'a perverted sadist'; she believes him to have been not a monster but (and this is presumably the purport of her rather cheap sub-title) an ordinary man. She goes carefully into the juridical foundations of the proceedings; she does not accept Mr. Pearlman's surprising description of the trial as 'due process of law', and she deplores in particular the politically directed attempt to combine with the prosecution of an individual a demonstration of what the Jewish race suffered at the hands of Hitler and his followers — an attempt that involved producing a huge volume of evidence concerning events with which the prisoner himself had little or nothing to do.

Dr. Arendt considers at some length, but only to reject them, objections to the proceedings based on their 'irregularities and abnormalities', contrasting these (not very clearly, however) with 'the central, moral, political and even legal problems that the trial inevitably posed'. She disposes, with a brisk *petitio principii*, of the objection that Eichmann was tried under a retroactive law, and dismisses (rightly, no doubt) any suggestion of 'the possible partiality of Jewish judges'.

[1] Hannah Arendt: *Eichmann in Jerusalem*. A report on the banality of evil. 275 pp. Faber and Faber.

She is not so happy about the kidnapping of the prisoner, suggesting that it might have been justified, or the Court's jurisdiction established (her argument does not seem quite coherent at this point), by a re-definition of the territorial principle on the basis 'that "territory", as law understands it, is a political and a legal concept, and not merely a geographical term'. Her argumentation here is a good example of the lengths to which her perverse cleverness can carry her. 'No State of Israel', she says, 'would ever have come into being if the Jewish people had not created and maintained its own specific in-between space throughout the long centuries of dispersion' — therefore Eichmann's crimes, in the eyes of the law, were committed (and he himself captured?) in Israeli territory: *Q.E.D.* Jurisprudence is evidently not Dr. Arendt's *forte*. She is on safer ground when she suggests that 'those who are convinced that justice, and nothing else, is the end of law will be inclined to condone the kidnapping act, though not because of precedents but, on the contrary, as a desperate, unprecedented and no-precedent-setting act, necessitated by the unsatisfactory condition of international law'. To accept this, however, is (as Dr. Arendt herself seems to be aware) to insert into the concept of the rule of law the thin end of a very penetrative wedge.

The most important juridical objection to the proceedings, in Dr. Arendt's opinion — and she believes it to be a valid one — is that Eichmann ought to have been tried by an international court, not because he did not obtain justice at the hands of his Israeli judges, but because his participation in genocide was a crime against humanity and not merely a crime (the crime of multiple murder) against the Jewish people: 'In so far as the victims were Jews, it was right and proper that a Jewish court should sit in judgment; but in so far as the crime was a crime against humanity, it needed an international tribunal to do justice to it.' Dr. Arendt admits that the actual court achieved without injustice 'its main purpose' — 'to prosecute and to defend, to judge and to punish Adolf

Eichmann'. But in her view the proceedings did not 'do justice' (ambiguous phrase!) to the offence that he had committed. Her argument appears to be that the exploitation of nuclear energy makes the threat of genocide today more terrifying than it has been in the past (but is the hydrogen bomb really capable of being used so selectively?), that it is therefore more than ever important for the human race to prevent a repetition of the crime, and that the judgment upon Eichmann would have been more effective to prevent such a repetition had it proceeded from an international tribunal. Surely the suggestion implies a mistaken view of what it is that in practice exercises a deterrent effect upon human beings. If recollection of the Eichmann case deters future generations from planning and participating in the crime of genocide, what will deter them will be the impression made upon them by the accumulated horror of the evidence and by a realization of the fate of the accused; the constitution of the court will neither add to nor detract from the effectiveness of the record.

Dr. Arendt devotes something like half her book to a survey of the various operations conducted against the Jewish people by the National Socialist regime, analysing in detail the process of deportation to the eastern killing centres from the Reich, from the Balkans, and from western and central Europe. Her object (in which she succeeds) is to show that the part played by Eichmann in these operations was a less authoritative one than that attributed to him by the prosecution, and that his attitude towards the whole process was very different from that depicted in the portrait painted by the Attorney-General in Jerusalem. Eichmann never killed with his own hands or gave direct orders for killing; his authority was limited to making arrangements for the supply of victims (by rail) and co-ordinating these arrangements in close cooperation with those actually in charge of the slaughter-houses; his desire was to be 'correct', to see that Jews were killed in an orderly and smooth-running fashion. Dr. Arendt also has no difficulty in showing that much of the evidence was related to operations in the east for which Eichmann's responsibility was, to say the least, dubious. Therefore Mr. Hausner's rhetorical attempt to call down upon his head the vengeance of six million persons, besides being founded, according to Dr. Arendt, upon a juridical fallacy (for it is the State, she insists, and not the victims, that should claim the penalty), was far from being justified by the evidence that he invoked in order to support it.

Dr. Arendt, then, 'cuts Eichmann down to size' and points out alleged juridical defects in the proceedings against him; but she goes farther than this. At times she seems to betray an excessive indulgence towards the artificers and executants of the Final Solution. She devotes several pages to expounding the thesis that extermination by gassing was a continuation of a policy of euthanasia already practised by the Nazis on the 'mentally sick' — implying, apparently, that this explains and in some measure condones the readiness of Germans to tolerate, and even, perhaps, their readiness to operate, this method of eliminating the Jewish race. She goes so far as to suggest that as the progress of the war made death and destruction and their concomitant horrors more and more familiar, 'the gassing centres in Auschwitz and Chelmno, in Majdanek and Belzek, in Treblinka and Sobibor must actually have appeared ['To whom?', one is tempted to ask — 'not, surely, to their inmates?'] the "Charitable Foundations for Institutional Care" that the experts in mercy death called them'. Eichmann himself, she suggests, 'was probably relieved' when this merciful method of extermination was substituted on an increasing scale for the crude murder by shooting practised by the Einsatzgruppen.

Eichmann may possibly have been relieved to learn of the improvement in method; he was, as Dr. Arendt insists, not a bloodthirsty monster but a cold-blooded official — indeed, it is this that makes him such a terrifying figure, the more because he was typical of hundreds of thousands of his compatriots. But if Eichmann was an official, he was a highly placed and very powerful one; he knew full well what went on in the Charitable Foundations, and on several occasions visited them and saw with his own eyes enough of their Institutional Care to make him physically sick, for he was a squeamish person; then he went back to the work of supplying them with human material for destruction, carrying out his task with undiminished diligence and even, in Hungary, prolonging it after the order had been given for the deportations to be halted. Dr. Arendt, for all her comprehension of his 'banality', does not suggest that when he was sent to the scaffold he met with anything more than his deserts.

There is another remarkable thing about Dr. Arendt's anxiety to understand the actors in her tragic drama: it is strangely eclectic; it does not extend, unfortunately, to all her fellow-Jews. Surveying the whole vast panorama of brutality and suffering that spread itself over Europe under Nazi domination, what is it that she, as a Jewish observer, finds 'the darkest chapter in the whole dark story'? Not the maniacal ruthlessness of Hitler and Goebbels and the 'racial' theorists; not the bestialities of Himmler and Streicher or the tyrannies of Kaltenbrunner and Hans Frank; not even the grisly business conducted by those who operated the gas chambers and the rest of the ghoulish apparatus of the extermination centres. No; for Dr. Arendt the 'darkest chapter' is the 'collaboration' of the Jews themselves with their destroyers. When she speaks of 'collaboration' (and that is the word she chooses regularly to employ) Dr. Arendt has not in mind the 'death-wish' that, according to the thesis of Bruno Bettelheim, deprived whole communities of the power and even the wish to resist; she is not thinking of the activities of the few real traitors (there are some such in every community) ready to buy survival or special treatment for themselves and their friends by betraying others to their death; she is referring generally to the conduct of the Jewish Councils set up by the Germans in the areas from which Jews were collected for deportation, and to the negotiations by Zionist leaders to procure permits for European Jews to escape to Palestine. All over Europe, in circumstances of varying horror, the only element common to them all being that the victims were utterly at the mercy of their captors, Jewish leaders did their best to negotiate some sort of terms to avert, or mitigate, or postpone, the common doom. Sometimes, no doubt, this involved the making of bargains that in the cold, safe light of today may appear ignoble. Dr. Arendt believes, or writes as if she believed, that in the eyes of a Jew the conduct of the Jewish Councils in these circumstances must be accounted worse than anything perpetrated by the Nazis.

It was this aspect of the book that aroused such bitter controversy when *Eichmann in Jerusalem* was first published in the United States; the pontifical rebukes of the League of B'nai B'rith, who pronounced it 'an evil book', were matched by the raptures of the self-consciously 'Gentile' Miss Mary McCarthy, who thought it 'splendid', and managed to detect in its pages 'a paean of transcendence, heavenly music, like that of the final chorus of *Figaro* or the *Messiah*'.

One does not have to be oneself a Jew — *pace* Miss McCarthy — to be both shocked and puzzled by this element in Dr. Arendt's book. Anyone, Jew or Gentile, can appreciate her skill in selecting and fitting together the most disparate and apparently insignificant pieces of evidence so that they compose a telling picture; but no one, Jew or Gentile, can fail to see that the picture is preconceived and the evidence chosen, and sometimes (no doubt unconsciously) distorted, in order to fit in with the preconception. Dr. Arendt writes as if her purpose were to launch, not directly but by innumerable insidious touches, a bitter attack upon the Jews caught up in the machinery of the Final Solution. Her main target is provided by the leaders of the Jewish Councils, who stood in an impossible position between their people and the persecutors;

they became, says Dr. Arendt in a sweeping and ambiguously loaded phrase, 'instruments of murder', they 'enjoyed their new power', and they played 'a great and disastrous role' in the destruction of their own people.

The items of evidence with which she constructs this picture hardly stand up to examination. She attacks at all levels. For instance, Dr. Leo Baeck, one of the most distinguished and deeply respected of the German Jewish leaders, who at an advanced age refused, in order to be with his people, to be evacuated from Berlin, is branded as being 'in the eyes of both Jews and Gentiles' the 'Jewish Führer' — and this simply (it appears) on the strength of his having once been so described by the infamous Nazi Wisliceny. The unhappy Dr. Kastner (he was afterwards murdered by an assassin who must have shared Dr. Arendt's opinion of his activities) does not escape her taunts: because he managed by negotiation to save the lives of some 1,600 Jews in Hungary, she contrives (by a dexterous transposition of poor Leo Gens's plea that 'with a hundred victims' he might 'save a thousand people') to suggest that Kastner was responsible for the deaths of all the Hungarian Jews who perished: 'Dr. Kastner', she sneers, 'saved exactly 1,684 people with 476,000 victims.'

Even the wretched Sonderkommandos, detailed for grisly duties in the killing centres, are made to appear worse than they really were: Dr. Arendt says at one point that they 'often' operated the 'extermination machinery' (an allegation quite unsupported by evidence); a few pages later 'often' becomes 'usually', and the unsupported allegation becomes a 'well-known fact'.

It is a constant theme of Dr. Arendt — and her belief in its truth is presumably the motivating force behind her whole attack — that if the Jews had refused to serve on the Councils and had resisted all attempts at organization, no large-scale massacres could have taken place. To suggest that the Jewish communities in Europe could have existed through those years of terror and privation without any organized leadership is quite unrealistic; and the resulting chaos would have involved suffering to no purpose, for lack of organization did not save nearly a million Jews in Soviet Russia from wholesale liquidation. Dr. Arendt's thesis, therefore, is at best a very questionable one; yet she asserts roundly that it contains 'the whole truth' and declares that the 'collaboration' of the Jewish leaders was evidence of 'total moral collapse' as striking as was the behaviour of their persecutors.

Why is it that this part of Dr. Arendt's book should seem so very shocking? The answer is not to be found by examining her premises or her arguments; it is her attitude that is at fault: her failure is a failure not of the intelligence but of imaginative understanding — the faculty that operates with her so freely when it is Eichmann himself that she is considering. When she is judging her less fortunate fellow-Jews, she writes as if she were quite unaware of the predicament in which they found themselves.

In her one published attempt at self-explanation, a letter in reply to a dignified protest from Professor Gershom Scholem, Dr. Arendt suggests that the right course for the millions of Jews in Europe (active resistance being, as she admits, out of the question) was simply *to do nothing*. 'And in order to do nothing', she proceeds, 'one needed only to say: I am just a simple Jew, and I have no desire to play any other role.' One has, surely, to be a very complicated Jew to suppose that, in practice, things were as simple for one's fellow-Jews as that.

It is one of the horrors of the present age that it has thrust upon the ordinary citizen the necessity of making choices of a kind that used to be familiar to us only from the pages of the historian or the casuist. Devotion to an ideology, especially under a totalitarian regime, has revived the horrors of the Inquisition and the old religious wars. Must you betray your family when your country's interests are at stake? Which comes first, the Party or your friend? Questions like these are no longer mere topics for debate in the schools, they have been

put to men and women, in situations of life and death, all over
Europe — and are still being so put to them farther east.
'There are some things a man should not do even to save his
country' — that is no longer mere rhetoric; each one of us may
be compelled to make out for himself his own list of such things
and to act upon his faith in it in the presence of a torturer or
with the knowledge that his friends and family are held as
hostages. Questions that, put to a witness by counsel, would be
deemed unfair, impossible to answer, were in occupied Europe
continually being asked, fair or unfair, by life itself, and they
had to be answered, one way or the other.

The impossible choice may present itself in many forms; here
is one that is taken from real life. A party of Jews was being
hidden from the police in the house of a Gentile; discovery
meant certain death not only for them but also for their pro-
tector; with the party was a baby, whose irrepressible wailing
was sure — the searchers were drawing near — to give their
hiding-place away. What was to be done? To allow the whole
party, the child included, to be consigned to extermination?
Or . . . ? Either course meant committing murder, of a kind.

That cruel dilemma may serve as a type of the situation in
which — with infinite varieties of circumstance and scale — the
leaders of the Jewish Councils found themselves. Even had they
had full knowledge of the facts and of their consequences, one
could not say that one course was the 'right' one for them to
take and the other the 'wrong'. The Jewish leaders for the most
part had no such knowledge; they had to act in the dark, with
only the light of their consciences to guide them. If ever there
was a case where the maxim 'Judge not' should be applied, or
where judgment should be informed by humility and imagination, it was surely here.

If Dr. Arendt's attitude towards those faced with such
dilemmas shocks the conscientious reader, it will also puzzle him.
Why is it that the fairness of mind that she displays, almost

ostentatiously, towards Eichmann and his associates apparently deserts her when she comes to deal with the leaders of the European Jews? Is it a case of 'falling over backwards' in two directions simultaneously? Of excessive anxiety not to be over-indignant in the one case, not to be over-indulgent in the other? Dr. Arendt is capable, one suspects, of such intellectual gymnastics; certainly she always gives one side, and never the other, the benefit of the doubt. An anti-Zionist attitude might explain why she is so bitter in her references to the activities of the Zionist agencies in occupied Europe; but that is only one part of the picture. Hostility to the policies of the State of Israel might account for the zest with which she girds at Mr. Hausner, the Attorney-General, and criticizes the conduct of the prosecution and the set-up of the trial; certainly the propagandist atmosphere so vividly reflected in Mr. Pearlman's book might well have provoked a violent reaction. But there is no apparent reason why such feelings should have been visited on the Jewish leaders faced with the horrors of the Final Solution.

Dr. Arendt, a woman of subtle intelligence, is of course aware of the other side of the picture she has chosen to paint of the part played by those who served on the Jewish Councils; a sensitive person, she must be capable of imagining the heroism displayed by many, the agony of mind and spirit endured by all. How then can she have brought herself to write them off all alike as 'collaborators', with no hint of sympathy for them in their suffering nor any word of admiration for the way in which the best of them endured it? One can hardly accept the bland extenuation offered by the egregious Miss McCarthy: 'the Jewish leadership are dead', she says, 'and beyond being hurt by [Dr. Arendt's slander], if it is a slander'; and all that she has said herself in answer to Professor Scholem on this point is that as a reporter of the trial she was not in a position to go outside the record: 'In my report I have only spoken of things which came up during the trial itself. It is for this reason that I could not mention the "saints" about whom you speak' — in other words, '*because* I only spoke of certain things, *therefore* I could not mention others'. Such an utterance suggests a problem of personality more puzzling even, perhaps, than that presented by Eichmann himself. It is worthy (might one say?) of Dr. Arendt's own powers of psychological analysis.

Both Dr. Arendt's volume and Mr. Pearlman's suggest a problem of which Eichmann's case is but a special instance: what judgment should be passed, not by the student of criminal or international law but by the moralist, upon those who conceived the Final Solution and those who carried it out? And which kind of participation, the planning or the execution, deserves to be the more strongly reprobated?

Before delivering a verdict in such a matter we should do our best, remembering the Christian precept, to understand the point of view of those that we are judging. The Final Solution was probably, it must be admitted, the most exacting and the most audacious enterprise ever embarked upon by the leaders of a nation. The problem that offered itself might well have been dismissed as insoluble: how to disinfect Europe of the evils engendered by a race that had insinuated itself like a host of deadly microbes into every class and every profession in each country, tightening its grip upon the social organism by intermarriage and the power of money, and numbering, in the area over which the operation was to be attempted, nearly eleven million individuals. How was it possible to cleanse society of a pest so ubiquitous and so deeply rooted? Various solutions had been put forward: first, deportation — to Palestine, to Poland, to Madagascar — then, when war closed those doors, concentration: the noxious tribe could be fenced off in special areas, while strict laws against intermarriage, reinforced by sterilization of the females of the species, safeguarded future generations from infection.

These measures, however, called for an exorbitant expenditure of time, labour, and money on the maintenance of camps and ghettos; moreover, they were at best makeshift expedients, for so long as there existed even a remnant of the Jewish race they were sure in the long run to reproduce themselves, like rabbits, and offer a constant threat to the purity of the Aryan breed. So Hitler, like Herod, decided to run no risks: there was nothing for it but complete elimination; eleven million human beings must be systematically put to death.

The difficulties that beset the execution of this project were of two kinds, the practical and the psychological. Collecting, classifying, transporting, and exterminating eleven million persons was a task that presented daunting logistic and administrative problems, and it speaks volumes for the organizing power and thoroughness of the Germans that they approached as nearly to their target as they did; the figure of six million was only attained by killing in the larger centres at the rate of 12,000 a day — an astonishing achievement, considering the difficulty of maintaining a steady flow of material in the face of military demands upon transport and manpower and the awkward subsidiary tasks undertaken such as cutting off hair, extracting teeth, and disposing of remains. The whole business called for widespread cooperation, both military and civil — and it was here that the psychological difficulty presented itself. The authorities had to ensure that the general public, and in particular those called upon to give active help, were favourably disposed, or at least not hostile, to an undertaking from which any decent, rational human being might have been expected to shrink with horror.

What proportion of the German people knew the truth about the Final Solution? And how much of the truth about it did they know? And if the full facts had been disclosed to the general public, what would their attitude have been? The answer that those then in power would have given to this last question is evident from the pains they took to conceal what was going on; they instituted an elaborate scheme of deception and employed a special vocabulary in order to preserve the façade: the Jews were being 'resettled', or 'rehabilitated', or removed to 'institutions for special treatment', and for words

such as 'liquidation' and 'extermination' (anything unequivocally signifying death was at all costs to be avoided) 'the Final
Solution' was itself the happy pseudonym. By this means not
only the public at large but the Jews themselves were protected
from knowledge of the painful truth, many of the deportees, it
appears, being put on to the death-trains in ignorance of what
was in store for them when they reached their destination.
Sometimes the merciful illusion was further prolonged: signs on
the railway-station suggested to new arrivals that they were
being welcomed to a holiday-camp or pleasure-resort, and even
the final selection of victims was accompanied by the strains
of classical music.

This procedure was not only useful for the purpose of deception; it also ministered to the national love of propriety, the
desire of the Germans to make everything as *nice* as possible,
their tendency to mask and mitigate (for themselves) the
existence of brutal facts by the use of abstract nouns. It thus
fulfilled a double function, concealing the truth from those
who did not know it, and disguising it for those who did. In all
official correspondence, even between those actually engaged in
organizing the holocaust, the polite fiction was maintained,
helping them to forget, or at least to overlook, the unpleasant-
nesses involved in the execution of their aim.

For those at the summit and at the centre of the organization,
farthest away from the actual doing of the grisly deeds, this feat
of forgetfulness or self-deception was easiest; for them a positive
effort of the imagination (though not, perhaps, an arduous one)
was needed if they were to envisage, in terms of suffering
human flesh, the horrors for which they made themselves responsible. No doubt they conceived it to be their duty not to
make that effort. If the means necessary for the achievement
of an object that you believe to be of high importance are such
that to contemplate them would lead you to waver in pursuing
it, or to abandon it entirely, are you to be blamed if you shut
your eyes to the horror of the means for the sake of achieving

the overriding aim? Ought Lenin to have counted the eggs he had to break in order to prepare his totalitarian omelette? Should Stalin have attempted to feel vicariously the sufferings of the Kulaks his policy compelled him to liquidate? Was it the duty (to take an instance nearer home) of a pilot embarking on a sortie of 'saturation' bombing to picture to himself the sufferings that would follow from the dropping of his cargo? Was it not rather his duty to restrain his imagination lest it should deter him from the execution of the necessary task?

Reflection upon questions such as these suggests that the guilt to be imputed to the architects of the Final Solution is not to be measured simply by the quantum of the suffering they inflicted, and that it is not mitigated by the fact that they believed their aim to be a good one; it lies in the evil of the aim itself; they must be judged ultimately by reference to the cause to which they dedicated themselves. Hypocrisy, brutality, the desire for personal or national aggrandisement, where they are present, afford material for further counts in the indictment; but honesty, kindheartedness, selfless devotion to his cause, will afford no defence on the main charge for one whose aim (even if he thinks it virtuous) is evil.

If it seems hard to condemn a man on moral grounds for an intellectual error in the choice of ends — he was after all (he may plead) only doing what he believed to be good — the answer is surely that the lie that betrays him is a lie in the soul; that the causes men dedicate themselves to (at any rate where their self-dedication is based on an intelligent evaluation of alternatives) reveal the kind of person that they really are. True, the weighing of ends against means — or of one end (for this is more often the real choice) against another — is not always easy, and a man is not necessarily to be branded as wicked simply because he has chosen wrong. But if a ruler commits himself to the belief that a certain end is so desirable that there is no need to count the cost of the human suffering (or of the sufferings of a particular race) involved in attaining it, he cannot expect indulgence from the moral arbiter who concludes that his aim, so far from justifying the use of evil means, was itself so wicked that it could have been conceived only by a monster or a madman.

The case is different with those who were mere executives; the horror we feel when we read of their doings is horror of a different kind — the simple horror inspired by man's inhumanity to man. Sadism apart — and we must conclude that there was plenty of inconceivably sadistic brutality in the Nazi camps, even if we allow for a degree of exaggeration on the part of witnesses — vindictive pleasure at the death, or the prospect of the death, of others is never, not even where it is felt in a good cause, an edifying emotion. 'Kill a good few for me!' said Miss Munro to her brother 'Saki', seeing him off to the Front in 1914; the sentiment, of course, was patriotic, but its utterance grates on a humane ear, like the applause that filled the Court in Moscow when sentence of death was passed on the unfortunate Penkovsky.

The staffs of the extermination camps were, of course, far more deeply involved than this; they were called upon not merely to applaud at a distance but actually to do things that no man, one might have hoped, could bring himself to do to other human beings. To marshal to their deaths, day after day, in circumstances of unimaginable degradation, hundreds and thousands of one's fellow-creatures — against that, flesh and blood, whatever the circumstances, must surely rise in irrepressible revolt. We all know the pleas in extenuation: at any sign of humanity on the part of the staff — a gesture of tenderness, perhaps, towards a child that refused to enter the gas-chamber by a different door from its mother, or an old man who faltered in digging his own grave, or a creature that, sniffing death like a steer in the Chicago stockyards, tried to break away from the procession to the human slaughterhouse — there would be at hand, no doubt, an under-officer with a revolver, vigilant to impose an impeccably 'objective' view of the situation. Orders, no doubt, were orders; and 'If I did not do it, another would'; the grim tasks must often have been undertaken with genuine reluctance and in the belief that they had to be performed in the interests of the common cause. The classic dilemma — 'There are some things a man should not do even to save his country' — again presents itself: if by so doing, and only by so doing, you could save humanity, would you kill, by slow torture, a hundred innocent human beings? or twenty? or two? or one? The question, it may be said, is not a fair one; but there is no guarantee that the world is so constructed that it could not present itself in practice, and it was in some such terms as these that the indoctrinated must have seen their situation. For them, indeed, the overriding aim was not the salvation of humanity, nor even the victory upon which they depended for their own survival, but simply a piece of social engineering that involved the elimination of a certain category of their fellow-men. The end was a monstrous one; but even if it had been as righteous as some of them at least believed it to be, ought any human being to have been a party to such means of bringing it about?

There are those who will find it all too easy to assess the blame to be allotted in such cases; others will find it difficult or impossible to judge at all. 'But we must judge': for those who believe in the existence of moral or of human values the obligation is inescapable.

The Press, Politics, and
Private Life

*

'We know of no spectacle so ridiculous', said Macaulay, 'as the British public in one of its periodic fits of morality'; and he proceeded to describe, in caustic language, the national tendency to indulge an outraged and 'outrageous' virtue at the expense of some unfortunate public man who has been convicted of an indiscretion that shocks its sense of decency. There has been in recent years no better example of these national explosions of 'outrageous virtue' than the affair that provoked the mixed crop of reports and commentaries now under review.[1]

Macaulay might have added that the British, when faced by the 'shocking' in life or literature, are inclined, after giving full vent to their indignation, to retreat from rational discussion of the phenomenon that excited it, protesting that they are bored by the whole business. It was thus that many persons, at the time of the controversy about *Lady Chatterley's Lover*, saved themselves from the embarrassment of saying what they really felt about the book by professing that they found it 'unreadable' — an expedient equally convenient for those who were

[1] *Lord Denning's Report*. 114 pp. H.M.S.O.
Wayland Young: *The Profumo Affair*. Aspects of conservatism. 118 pp. Penguin Books.
Iain Crawford: *The Profumo Affair*. A crisis in contemporary society. 176 pp. White Lodge.
Clive Irving, Ron Hall, Jeremy Wallington: *Scandal '63*. 227 pp. Heinemann.
Stephen Ward Speaks. Conversations with Warwick Charlton. 174 pp. *Today Magazine*. Odhams Press.
The Mandy Report. Illustrated. Confidential Publications.
Ludovic Kennedy: *The Trial of Stephen Ward*. 256 pp. Gollancz.

ashamed to admit that they were shocked by its outspokenness and for those who were ashamed to admit that they were not. The public complained with better reason that it was bored about the affair of Miss Christine Keeler, for the blatant vulgarity that assailed them on the subject week after week in the daily and the Sunday newspapers became very wearisome, and overlaid the real issues in the case. But the issues themselves were anything but boring, and now that the dust of controversy has settled it is worth while examining them and trying to see the whole affair in perspective and to set it in its proper place in contemporary political and social history.

What were, then, the underlying issues? If at the time it was not easy to identify them, that was not for want of mentors ready and eager to point out that they existed. Most of them seemed to agree that they lay in the field of ethics, and the Bishop of Southwark summed up a large volume of newspaper comment when he told a diocesan conference that 'Things have happened in recent weeks that have left an unpleasant smell — the smell of corruption in high places, of evil practices, and of a repudiation of the simple decencies and the basic values. . . . *The time has come* [reviewer's italics] *to clean the national stables*'.

The chorus of moral indignation was broken, it is true, by one or two obstinately questioning voices. One paper took a more robust view than most of its fellows: 'The Prime Minister', it said,

'is running a Government, not a monastery; the thunderous campaign being mounted to make one Minister's misbehaviour the occasion for a moral condemnation of Mr. Macmillan and the whole of his administration is the kind of organized hypocrisy which a healthy modern society can do better without'.

But the main burden of comment in the press was moral denunciation: Vice was rampant in High Places; the time had come for the Augean stables to be cleansed.

The Press, Politics, and Private Life

Looking back over the whole story in the light of the reports and commentaries now available, the detached observer may be inclined to agree that vice did reveal itself among those who occupied positions of power, and that there were several features of the affair that right-thinking persons might well consider shameful. But the vices and the persons who displayed them were not those at which the moral censors at the time pointed their accusing fingers. There is nothing in the evidence to confirm the suggestion that 'Society' (whatever nowadays that word may mean) is more vicious today than it was at any time in the past hundred years, or that 'Conservative circles' (another usefully ambiguous phrase) are more depraved than are the 'circles' of any other party. No: the most shameful feature of the Vassall and the Keeler stories — and the second of these stories cannot be fully understood unless it is considered in its relation to the first — was the unscrupulous procedure of a number of newspapers, which with an unctuous affectation of high-mindedness propagated rumours that were sure to stimulate the prurience of the public, regardless of the cost to the reputation of innocent individuals, of the Government services, and of the nation itself in the eyes of foreign observers. Two headlines, one of them published when Mr. Galbraith was under groundless suspicion of unduly intimate relations with his subordinate, the other appearing midway through the Keeler affair, may serve as examples of the depths to which the popular press descended at the time. 'MY DEAR VASSALL' was one newspaper's method of injecting a hint of homosexuality (always a titbit for the prurient) into what proved to be a perfectly innocent correspondence; 'PRINCE PHILIP AND THE PROFUMO SCANDAL' was the form of words with which another editor headed a column that loyally contrived at once to 'clear' and to smear the name of the Royal Family.

If moral condemnation was called for in connexion with the Vassall and Keeler cases it was surely on account of such performances as these; and the most interesting ethical problem

23

raised by either affair was not how to fix a proper standard for
the behaviour of public men, but how other responsible citizens
should react when a public man has apparently fallen short of
such a standard. The issue is one that confronts not the erring
politician but his critics: what, to put the question in a nut-
shell, are the circumstances that justify public criticism of
private lives?

'Civilization', according to an acute and liberal thinker, 'is a
thin and precarious crust erected by the personality and the will
of a very few and only maintained by rules and conventions
skilfully put across and guilefully preserved.' Whether or not
that has always been true of civilization in a large sense, it is
certainly the case that in civilized society today, at any rate in
this country, a fragile crust protects, and a tenuous curtain
conceals, the private life of the individual, in all walks of life
and at all social levels, from the gaze and criticism of the public.
The crust is thinner, the curtain less opaque, than in Victorian
days; the line it cuts through the nation does not coincide, as it
then practically did, with a line of social stratification that
divided London 'Society' from the country at large; but, in
spite of the breakdown of class barriers and the penetrative
assaults of wireless, of television, and of the popular press, the
curtain holds; and how resistant the crust can be when under
stress was shown most strikingly in the weeks that immediately
preceded the Abdication in 1936.

Some veil must be kept drawn to shield the privacy of the
individual if a civilized life is to be possible in a society that is at
once complex and libertarian. If those who 'guilefully preserve'
this veil may be thought to minister to a sort of hypocrisy, those
who seek to tear it aside in the name of truth or morality are
themselves often only humbugs of a higher and a holier kind.

Suppose that a journalist or politician has obtained convincing evidence about the private morals of a prominent man
which if disclosed would ruin his reputation and drive him,
perhaps for ever, from public life. The guilty secret need not

involve criminal liability; it is enough that it should be some
thing that would cast serious scandal upon his name. Rumours,
let us assume, are in circulation; this evidence would prove
them true. What use should the possessor make of the damaging
material?

Two conflicting answers are suggested: the first by those who
insist that the issue in such a case is essentially a moral one —
the school of thought represented by the newspapers already
referred to (one of which declared that Parliament should 'see
exposed and cleansed whatever there may be in this noxious
episode'), by the Bishop of Southwark, and by some at least of
the pack that hounded the late Minister for War from office;
the scandal, they insist, should not be covered up; the facts
should be brought into the light of day; the claims of Truth are
paramount.

The opposing school of thought maintains that in the
interests of society at large, no less than those of the individual
primarily concerned, the first duty of the possessor of such
evidence (even if he is a politician or a journalist) is to keep it
to himself; rather than lend his voice to the propagation of
rumour, he should do all he properly can to preserve unbroken
that façade on the maintenance of which depends the smooth
functioning not only of the social organism but also, so long as
ministries are manned by human beings and not by angels, of
the machine of government itself.

The more exalted the position of the individual whose conduct is impugned, the more sharply the issue is brought into
focus. Lapses on the part of a Lord Chancellor or a Prime
Minister, for instance, in this country, or of a President or a
Secretary of the State Department in the United States, are
more likely if bruited abroad to cause a serious public outcry
than are those of a minor official or a mere nonentity — the
more compelling, then, the duty to reveal the facts, according
to the first school of thought; the stronger the case for sup-
pressing them, according to the second.

To take a signal instance from the present century: it is now plain from the revelations published by his son that the adulteries of Lloyd George rendered him liable to an exposure that, given the moral code prevailing at that time, particularly among the Nonconformist ranks of his own party, must have driven him from office at a time when he was Prime Minister — perhaps even when he was presiding over the War Cabinet in the throes of our struggle with Germany. Many of his political opponents must have held the great man's future in the hollow of their hands. How plausibly they could have made 'security' and the liability to blackmail — apart from purely moral considerations — a pretext for his ruin! Yet not one of them betrayed him. Are his opponents to be blamed for failing to do their duty as citizens, vigilant to sustain the moral welfare of the nation, or do they deserve to be praised for sacrificing party advantage to its practical interests?

Those who deplore the hushing-up of moral delinquencies on the part of politicians will insist that a nation cannot afford to be served by men whose private lives will not stand up to the severest scrutiny. On the other side it may be said that a nation looking for public servants cannot afford to limit to such persons the ambit of its choice. Certainly it would not conduce to efficiency of administration if a blameless private life were deemed a necessary qualification for positions of public responsibility; such an ethical criterion would exclude from office many an outstandingly able man, and the impeccable morals of those who satisfied the test would hardly be a guarantee of their professional efficiency.

What is it, after all, that we really require of our public servants and our parliamentary representatives? Not, surely, that they should live spotless private lives (if they do, so much, from every point of view, the better), but that they should do their jobs efficiently and honestly, and should maintain in public the dignity and decency appropriate to their position. That a politician should be given to excessive drinking or that he should be a philanderer or an unfaithful husband is no doubt something that is for several reasons very much to be deplored; few people in twentieth-century England, however, would feel that he should therefore on moral grounds be excluded, or extruded, from the Government. But if he cannot keep sober in public, if he is always to be seen about with women of obviously low character and habits, or if his private failing is displayed in newspaper headlines or made the subject of political debate, then he is surely disqualified from high office not on moral grounds but on grounds of decency: the rulers and representatives of a great nation must — the requirement is almost an aesthetic one — maintain in the eye of the public an appropriate dignity. Appearances count.

If this is so, it is in a real sense true to say that the crime in such cases consists in being found out; and that the politicians or journalists who drag into the light of day the private weaknesses and peccadilloes of public men, so far from performing a meritorious action, are doing the nation a disservice by turning a private moral failing into a visible public blot; seeking to castigate one kind of offence, they are themselves accessories to the commission of another. Only some over-riding consideration of public policy can justify in such a case the breaking of the protective crust erected by civilized society.

It was said, indeed, that such overriding considerations existed in the case before us, and it was not the moral aspect of the matter, if their professions are to be taken at face value, that moved those who pressed in Parliament, in March and again in June, 1963, for an inquiry into the Keeler affair — though this did not prevent Mr. Harold Wilson from haranguing the House about the 'odious record', 'the sickness of an unrepresentative section of our society', and 'the moral challenge with which the whole nation is faced'. Their pretext on the earlier occasion was the rumour that the Minister for War had interfered with the course of justice by spiriting away Miss Keeler when she was due to give evidence in Court — an allegation in support of which it was found that there was 'no evidence whatever'. On the later occasion, after the Minister's confession, the pretext was what was loosely called 'the security aspect'; this also turned out to be a mare's nest.

Indeed, looking back, one wonders whether the public would ever have heard of the affair had not its circumstances, so heavily charged with possibilities of scandal, afforded an opening for the Opposition to aim a crippling blow at the prestige of the Government, for dissident Conservatives to attempt the discomfiture of the Prime Minister, and for the proprietors and editors of newspapers to set before their readers a feast of nauseating innuendo. But as soon as the matter was franked 'Security' those who wished for one reason or another to exploit it could do so with a clear conscience, or at least with a plausible excuse, however little danger to security in truth existed.

No one examining the evidence today is likely to conclude that Miss Keeler in fact ever obtained, or even asked for, any secret information from the Minister for War, let alone that she passed on any such information to the questionable Captain Ivanov. The popular picture of the British Minister and the Russian *attaché* sharing a mistress had obvious attractions for those who were in search of a scandal; but it turned out to be a figment, and it seems more than doubtful whether Miss Keeler ever had sexual relations with Ivanov at all. The question about 'warheads' that she said she had been asked to put to the Minister was a high-level question of policy, much canvassed in public: to suppose that it would have formed the subject of a spy's inquiry was, in Lord Kennet's phrase (in *The Profumo Affair*), 'a nonsense'; in any case, 'Nobody in their right senses', as Stephen Ward himself declared, 'would have asked somebody like Christine Keeler to obtain any information of that sort from Mr. Profumo — he would have jumped out of his skin.'

In short, no journalist or politician, however anxious about security, need have lost a moment's sleep in 1963 over the War Minister's brief liaison in 1961.

None the less, it may be said, there must have been a period of risk; and the real charge against the Government was that they did not detect and eliminate that risk through their Security Services. Was there not some fault in the organization or the functioning of the Services or in the handling by the Government of the information that reached it?

Part II of Lord Denning's report explains in detail how the Security Services are organized and how they operated in the present case; it traces, step by step, in fifty factual paragraphs (paragraphs 230–277) the whole complicated story; and its vindication of the Services is complete. In 1961, says Lord Denning (paragraph 34), they did not know of the Minister's affair with Miss Keeler 'and had no reason to suspect it', and by the time the matter blew up in 1963 it had ceased to be a 'security interest' (paragraph 267). True, the Services had in their possession early in February, 1963, two police reports containing (*inter alia*) statements by Miss Keeler to the effect that she had had eighteen months previously 'an association' with the Minister for War and that Ward had asked her to obtain secret information from him, and they did not pass on these reports to the Prime Minister's office until the end of May. This delay is the only plausible target for criticism of their handling of the affair: 'The real charge against Mr. Macmillan', say the authors of *Scandal 1963*, 'by now obscured by the flood of moral cant and political skullduggery, was that it had taken 123 days for one document to pass from the security authorities to Admiralty House.' But the Security Services, as Lord Denning makes plain, were behaving in accordance with the directive defining their duties, which laid down that they should take action only in a case where a risk to security actually existed. They rightly discounted the story about Ward's request for information concerning 'warheads'; 'There was no suggestion that Christine Keeler had complied with the request, or that Mr. Profumo had ever given her any such information (paragraph 267); and as for the bare fact of the Minister's past association with her, that, whatever its

political significance as a moral lapse on the part of a member
of the Cabinet, was no longer a security interest, and in any
case it was already known to Admiralty House, and the
Minister (as the Security Services were aware) was being directly
confronted with the matter by the Attorney-General and the
Chief Whip.

We turn therefore to the critics' third line of attack: even if
there was no actual 'leak', even if there was no real risk, the
Government's handling of the matter, it was said, was such as
to call for a full inquiry; they had forfeited the confidence of
the country, declared Mr. Grimond in the House, and should
resign forthwith. The wildest accusations were freely uttered:
the Prime Minister was lying; he had known the truth all
along; if he had not known it, he ought to have; the Minister
for War should have been 'watched' (by the Security Services?
by the police?) back in 1961; his colleagues should never have
accepted — nay, they did not really believe — his denial of his
guilt; at best, the story revealed a shocking record of apathy
and carelessness, at worst, a conspiracy to shield 'the Conservative establishment'.

Most of the cries raised at the time have now a hollow ring;
no one really supposes that Mr. Macmillan was lying, or that
the police should spend their time shadowing Cabinet Ministers
at cocktail parties and at night clubs; such totalitarian pro-
cedures, even if they guaranteed (and would they?) perfect
security, would involve a price too high for a free society to pay.
But the charge that the Ministers were culpable in believing
their colleague's assurances still persists, and the scornful
criticisms that were levelled at them then for their gullibility
(or worse), based largely on a misconception of the nature and
circumstances of the famous 'midnight' meeting, are echoed in
some of the publications that are before us now. At this point
even Mr. Iain Crawford, usually a reliable reporter, goes quite
astray.

It would of course be unrealistic to suggest that when a

question of confidence arises no Cabinet Minister should ever suspect a colleague of untruthfulness; history provides all too many examples of statesmen who have failed to maintain a proper standard of integrity. Yet, even when all appearances are against the suspect, even when his colleagues feel in their bones that he must be guilty, still, if he backs up his repeated denials of his guilt by declaring his readiness to submit to cross-examination in the Courts and actually takes steps towards initiating a prosecution, what alternative have they but to accept his word — on which in this case he set his seal by offering solemnly to repeat his denial in the House of Commons? Of the two improbabilities before them which is the more improbable? To accept it as more likely that a Minister in such circumstances should deceive his colleagues would be to acknowledge, and in a sense to be a party to, a debasement of the currency of public life.

Apart therefore from the moral issue in which the Opposition officially disclaimed all interest, there was no solid substance in the case. What then were the motives of those who pressed so eagerly, in Parliament and the press, for an inquiry?

No doubt as on all such occasions they were mixed. It is suggested in more than one of the books before us that they included an element of vindictiveness: the press (it is said) were eager (as well they might have been) to avenge the searing exposure they had suffered at the hands of the Radcliffe Tribunal in the Vassall case, while the Opposition saw a heaven-sent opportunity of harassing the Government. All the accounts before us agree that Mr. Wigg, who felt that he had suffered unjustly at Mr. Profumo's hands not long before in an exchange about Kuwait, acted from the beginning as the whipper-in of the Opposition pack. As early as December, 1962, a friend of his, one Lewis, between whom and Ward 'there was' (in Lord Denning's words) 'no love lost', learnt from Miss Keeler of her association with the Minister for War, and (again to quote Lord Denning) he thenceforward 'kept Mr. Wigg informed of every development. They had conversations

31

almost daily'. Lewis 'was so interested that he, in March, 1963, got his own agent to investigate in the person of a journalist who spent much time in Stephen Ward's flat'. Journalists at this time, in a more familiar but no less repugnant exercise of their *métier*, were thronging the doorsteps of the principal parties in the affair; Ward himself was compelled to call for the police to protect himself from their attentions, and Mr. and Mrs. Profumo had to fight their way through a crowd of them in order to get into their house after midnight. Meanwhile Miss Keeler had sold, and a newspaper had bought, her own 'story' of her association with the Minister and the 'effusive but not conclusive' letter that he addressed to her. Plainly, the truth could not long remain concealed, and the Minister's solemn denial of it in the House of Commons — an inexcusable act, though the circumstances in which his statement came into being go far to explain his conduct, if not to mitigate his guilt — presented the Opposition with his head — and, it seemed, the Government's also — upon a charger.

Whatever personal or party feelings may have moved Mr. Wigg and his colleagues, they no doubt believed the charges they so freely launched against their opponents. Indeed, the worst that can be safely said about them — and it is surely bad enough — is not that they did not believe in the truth of their indictment, but that they did. There was indeed hardly any baseness with which Mr. Wigg was not prepared to credit the Government and its members. 'A lying humbug' was his reiterated description of the Minister who was loudest in repudiating his unhappy colleague, and his opinion of the Government collectively may be gathered from a question that he asked when news of the tragic death and gruesome mutila-tion of two British soldiers in the Middle East had reached England and was awaiting confirmation: 'Is it not a fact that Government circles did all they could to boost the story in the hope that it was true?' That is a question that tells one more about the individual who asked it than it tells about those at whom it was directed; one can often judge a man's own standards by observing what standards he imputes to others; one who could believe that to be a fact could surely believe anything of his political opponents; and 'sincerity' of a sort may have characterized even the wildest of the charges that the Opposition flung at the Government in the course of the Keeler debates.

It was in such an atmosphere and by agents so motivated that the train of events was set in motion that led directly to the downfall of the Minister for War and indirectly to the death of Stephen Ward.

The affair engendered a mixed crop of 'literature', ranging from Lord Denning's Report (surely the raciest and most readable Blue Book ever published), through ephemeral 'revelations' of the kind that went to make up the cloudy atmosphere of the case, to catch-penny paperbacks rushed out by opportunist commentators while interest in the scandal was still warm. Samples of all these kinds are before us. Some of them are truly revealing documents; others are so slanted that they prove nothing but the prejudices of their authors. Among these last must be counted *The Profumo Affair* by Wayland Young (Lord Kennet). Its sub-title 'Aspects of Conservatism' sufficiently reveals its character and purpose; it makes the 'Affair' a spring-board for an out-and-out attack upon the Conservative 'establishment'. The author's attitude is vividly conveyed by a sentence that he quotes from an article written at the time:
'For the sake of our children and all that we hold in regard we can no longer uphold the polluted mentality of those who claim "we are born to lead" — in other words the doubtful spawn of Eton and Harrow, who too often have exercised power in our land.'

Lord Kennet trains his guns not only upon the 'public-school Tories' and 'the intellectual lackeys to whom they are put out for education', but upon Conservatives at large: 'In the Profumo affair', he concludes, 'the political frivolity, moral myopia, and the herd-credulity of latter-day Toryism led to convulsion and the sacrifice of one life, one career, and several reputations.' Plainly, one does not go to the writer of that sentence for a factual account of the episode or a balanced judgment of its implications.

A more factual account and a more balanced judgment are to be found in *The Profumo Affair* by Mr. Iain Crawford. Mr. Crawford is well informed, sensible, and shrewd, and betrays no *parti pris*. His pompous sub-title, 'A Crisis in Contemporary Society', was perhaps imposed on him by his publishers, who are no doubt also responsible for a deplorable blurb; it belies his treatment of the subject, which is colloquial without being cheap. But though the book is written with an eye to a contemporary audience, it has evidence to offer to future historians of the affair, including some inside information about the activities of Mr. Wigg, a feature that it shares with *Scandal 1963*, an otherwise ephemeral production, whose quality is pretty accurately indicated by its title.

Mr. Charlton's brochure belongs frankly to the category of 'revelations'; its author is a journalist who evidently gained Ward's intimacy and enjoyed (like Mr. Lewis's agent) a series of conversations with the osteopath in his flat. Mr. Charlton does his best — an experienced reporter's best — to present an attractive portrait of his subject. But the impression that remains is that Ward, though certainly not mercenary where sex was concerned, was an unprepossessing individual, one of whose principal pleasures was to procure pretty girls and get them to undress in front of his friends.

The Mandy Report, like Lord Denning's, is a primary document for students of the affair; Lord Denning provides the facts, Mandy supplies the atmosphere. As an authentic picture of the background, her confessions are worth their weight in mink. Her voice and personality repeatedly break through the blanket imposed by the ghost-writer, whether she is describing 'Life with my first millionaire' ('a dream come true for a girl who was hardly 16') or giving her reasons for going back to her second: 'After a lot of heart searching and

some simple arithmetic I decided to return to live with Peter
Rachman.' Her own, too, surely, are the descriptions of
interior decoration — the 'Renoir-style paintings' of Mr.
Charles Clore ('Do not misunderstand me — we were not dining
alone') and the glories of her own 'beautiful little place': 'The
lounge was decorated in a pale rose colour and had antique gas
lamps. A gold Welsh harp stood in one corner and there was a
large, modern three piece suite in green and gold.'

Apart from the interest it gains from its political context, the
story of the girl from Solihull and her adventures in Mayfair
and at Cliveden is of real value as a social document; but Miss
Rice-Davies, though she protests no doubt sincerely that she is
'not a hypocrite or a liar', is something of a prude, and her
concern for her reputation deprives her record at certain points
of credibility. 'Thank heavens for one thing', she says, describing her experience in Holloway, 'at least I was in a cell of my
own away from the Lesbians to be found all over the jail. So I
never had to fight for my honour on top of all my other
problems.' Again: 'I am an expensive courtesan if you like, but
never a prostitute. I have never had to raise a finger or bare a
knee to capture any man.' She clings through thick and thin,
and she has had plenty of both, to what she calls her honour —
better described perhaps as her reputation for sexual in-
dependence. So, though we may believe her when she tells us
that Dr. Ward 'never did anything for nothing', for it tallies
with all the other evidence, it is another matter when she
protests that she never slept with other men at his request.

Mr. Ludovic Kennedy, in *The Trial of Stephen Ward*, seizes
too readily on this last assertion in Miss Rice-Davies's 'Report',
because it serves his main purpose, which is to prove that
Ward's conviction was the result of a miscarriage of justice.
His book is an eye-witness account of the trial, giving the
author's impressions of the Judge, counsel, and witnesses, and
his opinions on the procedure and the law applicable to the
case. Mr. Kennedy spoils his account by his manner of present-
ing it, and weakens the effectiveness of his plea for Ward by his

unremitting prejudice. As a reporter — apart from an idio-
syncratic use of English: we meet 'a mutual peer' (evidently a
common friend of Mr. Kennedy and Ward) and six pages later
'a tight concentric circle' — he is too bright, too knowing, too
facetious; he cannot be content to report: Miss Keeler is a
'nymph'; Dr. Ward is a 'screaming hetero'; the jury are almost
invariably 'the rude mechanicals'; one poor girl who gave
evidence is 'in officers' mess parlance, a ten bob knock in the
Bayswater Road' (what officers' messes, one wonders, can Mr.
Kennedy be thinking of?), and when counsel begins a question
'Do you remember . . . ?' Mr. Kennedy cannot help telling us
that 'for one mad moment I thought he was going to say "an
inn, Miranda".' Sometimes this facetiousness seems to be due
to spontaneous exhibitionism, the author simply cannot help
showing off his whimsical humour, but more often it has a
practical purpose: he is out to pour ridicule upon the prosecution or upon the whole proceedings.

For Mr. Kennedy is, understandably, impatient of British
judicial procedure — the elaborate formalities, the archaic
dress, the traditionally stilted language, the conventional and often
outdated attitude on moral questions adopted by the law
and some of those who administer it, and (in particular) the
apparent irrationality of many of the rules of evidence. 'The
archaic ritual', he writes, 'is positively harmful. . . . A small
reform like the shedding of horsehair would be a step in the right
direction. . . . Judge and counsel would be seen to be human
too.' So far, perhaps, so good; but he goes on: 'Let no one
pretend that our system of justice is a search for truth. It is
nothing of the kind. It is a contest between two sides played
according to certain rules, and if the truth happens to emerge as
the result of the contest, then that is pure windfall. But it is
unlikely to.' There is an element of truth in this, but Mr.
Kennedy spoils his case by allowing his feelings to get the better
of his reason. Certainly the rules of evidence in criminal proceedings are highly artificial, and there is a case, which many
lawyers would support, for reforming them; elaborate regula-

tions, at almost every trial, exclude a great deal of the truth. But these regulations have been developed in the interests of the prisoner, and the loosening-up desired by Mr. Kennedy, if it meant more justice, would mean justice of a rougher kind; it would result in the conviction of many guilty men, and perhaps some innocent men, who under the present system would have been acquitted.

When it comes to Lord Denning's inquiry Mr. Kennedy's *penchant* for informality deserts him. No doubt in the relaxed atmosphere of the Master of the Rolls's study (no horsehair there, except perhaps in the upholstery) much more of the truth came out than could emerge in Court, and in deciding what to accept and what to reject Lord Denning was not hampered by any archaic or artificial rules; but Mr. Kennedy takes him to task precisely because, in his admirably human and common-sense report, he accepted evidence that bore the stamp of truth although it had not passed the rigid tests that would have had to be applied to it in Court.

Ward was certainly the victim of a terrible misfortune, but it is hard to believe that he suffered an actual injustice. He might well have claimed that he ought never to have been put on trial, but not — in spite of all the play that Mr. Kennedy makes with conflicting evidence and anomalies of procedure   that the result of his trial was an unjust one.   After all, he was acquitted on all but two of the charges he was tried on — where there was doubt, the jury evidently allowed him the benefit of it — and on those two charges (living on the earnings of Miss Keeler and Miss Rice-Davies) the defence offered no evidence but the prisoner's, which even Mr. Kennedy finds, on this issue, impossible to believe: Ward's profession of 'horror' at hearing that Miss Keeler accepted money for her services was, too plainly, simulated. And the jury may well have asked themselves why the defence failed to call the sinister Indian doctor, or Lord Astor, whose testimony, as the Judge observed, *if Ward was telling the truth* (a qualification that his apologists are inclined to forget, or to suppress), might well have helped to save him. Whether, in 1961, he actually needed money from the girls is not relevant, and even if it were, Mr. Kennedy does nothing to help Ward's case by pointing out that at the time of the trial in 1963 his drawings were selling for £500. Ward was obviously not above pocketing some of the earnings of his girls when he was hard up — after all, he himself provided for them generously — and in the circumstances of the case that was enough to justify a conviction.

But Ward was certainly not the kind of professional that the Sexual Offences Act was aimed at, the runner of a profitable call-girl racket; his object was not money but sex for its own sake; the intimate glimpses given by Mr. Charlton and Miss Rice-Davies leave no doubt of that; 'sex', indeed, had so long and so deeply obsessed him that his palate had become jaded; hence the 'vibro', the whippings, the nude parties, the 'four-in-hands', all of them well-attested variations that added a necessary spice to his every-day, or every-night, enjoyments.

But it was not for indulgences such as these that Ward was being tried, and the criminal element in his behaviour, assuming it proved, was so trivial that one hopes that his sentence, if he had lived to receive it, would have been a light one — a possibility that adds a touch of irony to his suicide.

Why, then, was Ward put on his trial? Mr. Kennedy's answer, and it is an answer very generally accepted, is that he was 'a whipping-boy for the humiliations of the Government', the scape-goat of the Establishment; that he suffered for the sins of the Society that he pandered to, the Society that deserted him in his hour of need.

That is an easy answer, and one very comforting to critics of 'the Establishment', but it does not quite make sense. For it presupposes a decision taken for political reasons and presumably at the highest level, and an incredibly foolish one at that: the Cabinet (one is apparently asked to believe) decided to prosecute in order (to quote Mr. Kennedy) 'to help restore the Government's good name'. One can only say that if the Cabinet (or any other authoritative body) had the issue before it, and decided it on these grounds, they were guilty of a strange miscalculation; for it is hard to see how anybody's face, least of all the Establishment's, was to be saved by the washing in public of so much dirty linen, some of it marked with embroidered coronets. No: the true answer to the question appears from Lord Denning's Report: the decision to investigate Ward's activities was taken by the Commissioner of Police, and it was forced upon him by anonymous communications received by the C.I.D. alleging that Ward was living on the immoral earnings of girls '*and suggesting that he was being protected by his friends in high places*' (paragraph 200). The investigations so called for disclosed evidence which, to say the least, was (as events proved) adequate to secure a conviction. What would have been said of the Commissioner, of the Home Secretary, of the Government, if in these circumstances the authorities had failed to prosecute? Surely, that once more the Establishment had closed its ranks, that 'Conservative circles' were shielding their protégé, and themselves, from the disclosures that would be bound to follow if he faced an indictment in open court. And who would have been the foremost to launch those charges? The very newspapers, the very politicians, who at the time were clamouring for an inquiry into the affair and now seek to saddle others with the blame for its results. If Ward was a victim of anything other than a concatenation of unfortunate coincidences, he was sacrificed not to the convenience of the Government but to the clamours of its critics. His case is but one more example of the sacrifice of the private life of the individual in the supposed interests of the public; it was his peculiar misfortune that he forfeited not merely privacy but life itself.

Regina v. Penguin Books Ltd.:
An Undisclosed Element in the Case

*

I have recently had occasion to study the Penguin summary of the proceedings in the *Lady Chatterley* prosecution, and to read with close attention the unexpurgated version of the novel. As I perused *Lady Chatterley's Lover*, the significance of certain passages in the book, not obvious at a first reading, gradually became clear to me; and these passages, once their true meaning was appreciated, revealed an unsuspected element in Lawrence's beliefs and feelings about sex — something that one would, I think, be justified in calling a most important tenet in his sexual creed. Yet, if the Penguin summary is to be trusted, this remarkable belief of Lawrence's was not once referred to in the course of the Old Bailey proceedings (although the trial provided, according to the publishers, Penguin Books Ltd., 'probably the most thorough and expensive seminar on Lawrence's work ever given'), and the passage that contains the fullest revelation of it — a passage which is a climax, if not *the* climax, of the novel — was referred to by only one of the thirty-five 'experts' who gave evidence about the book, and that witness did not explain its significance — if, indeed, he understood it.

Towards the end of the trial, it is true, attention was drawn to this very passage, not by a witness but by prosecuting counsel, who read parts of it to the jury in the course of his closing speech, with the cryptic comment, 'Not very easy, sometimes, not very easy, you know, to know what he is driving at.' But though counsel no doubt himself appreciated what Lawrence was 'driving at', he did not explain it to the jury, and was content to leave the matter there.

40

An Undisclosed Element in the Case

As for the defence, even if they fully appreciated the meaning of the passage, they were of course under no obligation to refer to it if they thought that such a reference would be harmful to their case; the duty of defending counsel was owed not to Literature but to their clients, Penguin Books Ltd., whose considerable financial interest in the book involved them in their turn in a duty to their shareholders. Anyhow, Mr. Gerald Gardiner made no reference to the matter in the very full account that he gave to the jury of the sexual element in the novel; and, naturally, neither side having made any point of it, there was no reference to it in the Judge's summing-up.

Now that the case is over and the shareholders are secure in enjoyment of their profits, Penguin Books would no doubt be the first to agree that it is in the interests of Literature that Lawrence's full meaning and purpose in the book should be made clear to its readers.

The passages — for there are more than one of them — that so surprisingly escaped notice at the Old Bailey reveal Lawrence's attitude towards a certain 'unnatural' sexual practice. Lawrence weaves into his story not merely a defence but a panegyric of this practice, making *Lady Chatterley's Lover* a vehicle for conveying his belief that it is a proper, if not a necessary, element in a full sexual relationship between man and woman.

It is best, at the outset, to be clear about the meaning of the words we have to use. The practice approved by Lawrence is that known in English law as buggery. This is by no means to be equated (as is sometimes ignorantly supposed, and as colloquial usage might suggest) with homosexual practice. 'Homosexual relations' means sexual relations between men or between women; under our law, any indulgence in such relations between men (assuming that it constitutes an act of 'gross indecency') is an offence punishable by not more than two years' imprisonment; between women, such indulgence is no offence at all. The 'full offence' of buggery, on the other hand, involves *penetratio per anum;* here, the active party can only, of course, be a man; the passive party may be either a man or a woman; in either case, both parties (even if husband and wife) are liable under our law to imprisonment for life.

There is no need here to discuss whether indulgence in these practices is morally wrong, or how wrong it may be, or whether all or any of them should be forbidden by law — the answers to these questions are irrelevant to my present purpose.

Nor do I attempt to answer the question whether *Lady Chatterley's Lover* was 'obscene' within the meaning of the Obscene Publications Act, 1959, under which the proceedings against the book were taken; nor the question whether, if it was obscene, its literary or other merits are such as would have justified an acquittal under the Act; the answers to these questions are likewise irrelevant to the point I seek to bring to light. But, though it is not my purpose to criticise either the trial or the book itself, I ought perhaps to confess that to me the defence reeked of humbug (I do not say hypocrisy, for all the witnesses were no doubt sincere, however much of their evidence may appear ridiculous or pathetic to a dispassionate observer), and that I find the novel extremely distasteful, despite its serious purpose and the brilliance of a number of passages in it, and think it a failure both as a moral or sociological tract and as a work of art. But Lawrence was beyond question important as a writer and as a proponent of sexual reform, and it seems worth while to bring into the light of day what is, if I am right, an important article in his sexual creed.

'If I am right': I can only appeal, in support of my thesis, to the text.

A main theme of Lawrence's novel is the sexual relationship between Lady Chatterley and the gamekeeper Mellors, and the change wrought in Lady Chatterley herself by the attentions of an expert — for whatever else Mellors may have been, Lawrence leaves us in no doubt that he was that. Lawrence carried out this part of his purpose by describing nine meetings between the lovers,[1] on eight of which occasions they perform (on two of them, three times) the sexual act. He describes in varying degrees of detail both the act and the sensations (particularly the woman's) that accompany it, and these descriptions contain remarkable *tours de force* of imaginative and poetical writing.

It was suggested by the prosecution that the author's object in so fully and repeatedly describing sexual intercourse was little or no better than pornographic: that he was pandering to the prurience of his readers, that 'sex' was dragged in for its own sake, and that the rest of the book was little more than padding. This was met with an uncompromising denial by the other side. The first witness for the defence, Mr. Graham Hough, put the matter thus (*Trial*, p. 44):[2]

'The reason for the repeated descriptions of sexual scenes is to show the development of Connie Chatterley's awareness of her own nature. The scenes are not the same, they are not repetitive; they are different, and this is a very important part of Lawrence's purpose.'

The assertion that each sexual scene plays its special part in a carefully planned development was reiterated both by the leading counsel for the defence and by his witnesses. 'The physical relations between (Lady Chatterley) and the man,' said Mr. Gardiner (*Trial*, p. 31), 'so far from being a repetition, are a slow steady development'; 'Any good reading of the book,' said Mr. Richard Hoggart (*Trial*, p. 95), 'I don't mean a highbrow's reading, a good decent person's reading of the book, shows there is no one the same as the next; each one is a progression of greater honesty and a greater understanding'; and Miss Janet Adam Smith (*Trial*, pp. 156–7) declared that these descriptions were 'very relevant and necessary to the theme. They show,' she continued, 'the two characters having an increasing awareness of each other.'

---

[1] Not counting two occasions on which Sir Clifford is present.
[2] My references throughout are to the Penguin edition of the novel ('*L.C.*') and to the Penguin summary of the Old Bailey proceedings ('*Trial*').

Of these two views about the book, the defence's was surely, in the main, the right one: Lawrence's concern with sex was the reverse of prurient or pornographic; the full descriptions of the sexual act were inserted as a serious literary experiment; and no doubt each episode was introduced in order to show its effect upon Lady Chatterley's awareness of her own sexual nature. But it cannot really be maintained that (as the 'experts' quoted above would have us think) the series represents a steady progression, each episode being accompanied by an increase in mutual awareness; rather, Lawrence seems to be anxious to show that varying moods, and changes in currents of feeling of which the individual is not always conscious, may so affect him (or her) that today's act of intercourse, even between devoted lovers, may be less satisfying both physically and emotionally, and less 'revealing,' than yesterday's.

None the less, it certainly appears from a study of the text that Lawrence had a special purpose in introducing each of the eight 'sexual' episodes. There is no need to describe each of these episodes in detail; briefly, on the first two occasions (*L.C.*, pp. 120–1, 130–1) the pleasure is almost entirely the man's; it is not until the third encounter (*L.C.*, pp. 138–9) that the experience is a success, both physically and emotionally, for the woman also; the next act of intercourse (*L.C.*, pp. 178–9) is, from the woman's point of view, a miserable failure, but it is followed on the same occasion by two blissful consummations (*L.C.*, pp. 180–3); the fifth occasion (*L.C.*, pp. 217–22) provides opportunity for three acts of intercourse and much sexual talk, which certainly teaches Lady Chatterley a good deal that she did not know before about the person — if not the personality — of her lover. The sixth episode (*L.C.*, p. 231) is a ridiculous animal romp in a rainstorm: 'He tipped her up and fell with her on the path, in the roaring silence of the rain, and short and sharp he took her, short and sharp and finished, like an animal.'

The significant episode, for my purpose, is the seventh,

described by Lawrence as 'a night of sensual passion' (*L.C.*, p. 258). It comes (to quote Mr. Andrew Shonfield),[1] 'at the very climax of the sexual relationship between Mellors and Lady Chatterley . . . when they spend a night together, before her departure for Italy, and he "burns out the shame" in her. He does this' (says Mr. Shonfield) 'by various feats of love-making which are undescribed, though we are left in no doubt that what Mellors did was unconventional and even perverse' — and Mr. Shonfield goes on to speculate on the precise kind of perverse sexual treatment that Lady Chatterley had been subjected to, concluding that 'it seems a reasonable guess' that she was made the victim of 'the same anal perversion' that Mellors' wife, a little later on in the book, says he had practised on her years before.

It can be shown conclusively, I think, by reference to the text, (1) that it is not merely 'a reasonable guess' but an absolute certainty that this was what happened on the 'night of sensual passion'; (2) that Lawrence, though he chose to depend on hints, innuendoes, and half-hidden clues, meant to leave a careful reader in no doubt about the matter; and (3) that he left in the book equally unequivocal evidence that he himself approved of the practice in question, where the passive party was a woman.

The care that Lawrence took, in his thrice-written novel, to insert (and half-hide) this series of clues, the climactic position he gave to the crucial episode, and the seal of approval he set upon it, all go to show the importance he attached to the matter, and justify a full quotation of his account of the episode itself (pp. 258–9):

'It was a night of sensual passion, in which she was a little startled and almost unwilling: yet pierced again with piercing thrills of sensuality, different, sharper, more terrible than the thrills of tenderness, but, at the moment, more desirable. Though a little frightened, she let him have his way, and the

---

[1] See '*Lawrence's Other Censor*', in ENCOUNTER, September 1961, p. 63.

reckless, shameless sensuality shook her to her foundations, stripped her to the very last, and made a different woman of her. It was not really love. It was not voluptuousness. It was sensuality sharp and searing as fire, burning the soul to tinder.

'Burning out the shames, the deepest, oldest shames, in the most secret places. It cost her an effort to let him have his way and his will of her. She had to be a passive, consenting thing, like a slave, a physical slave. Yet the passion licked round her, consuming, and when the sensual flame of it pressed through her bowels and breast, she really thought she was dying: yet a poignant, marvellous death.

'She had often wondered what Abélard meant, when he said that in their year of love he and Héloise had passed through all the stages and refinements of passion. The same thing, a thousand years ago: ten thousand years ago! The same on the Greek vases, everywhere! The refinements of passion, the extravagances of sensuality! And necessary, forever necessary, to burn out false shames and smelt out the heaviest ore of the body into purity. With the fire of sheer sensuality.

'In the short summer night she learnt so much. She would have thought a woman would have died of shame. Instead of which, the shame died. Shame, which is fear: the deep organic shame, the old, old physical fear which crouches in the bodily roots of us, and can only be chased away by the sensual fire, at last it was roused up and routed by the phallic hunt of the man, and she came to the very heart of the jungle of herself. She felt, now, she had come to the real bed-rock of her nature, and was essentially shameless. She was her sensual self, naked and un-ashamed. She felt a triumph, almost a vainglory. So! That was how it was! That was life! That was how oneself really was! There was nothing left to disguise or be ashamed of. She shared her ultimate nakedness with a man, another being.

'And what a reckless devil the man was! really like a devil! One had to be strong to bear him. But it took some getting at, the core of the physical jungle, the last and deepest recess of organic shame. The phallus alone could explore it. And how he had pressed in on her!

'And how, in fear, she had hated it. But how she had really wanted it! She knew now. At the bottom of her soul, fundamentally, she had needed this phallic hunting out, she had secretly wanted it, and she had believed that she would never get it. Now suddenly there it was, and a man was sharing her last and final nakedness, she was shameless.

'What liars poets and everybody were! They made one think one wanted sentiment. When what one supremely wanted was this piercing, consuming, rather awful sensuality. To find a man who dared do it, without shame or sin or final misgiving!'

What does one particularly remark in this account of Lady Chatterley's feelings? Surely, that there is nowhere any reference to the 'sex thrill' (as Lawrence calls it) so fully described as the climax of her reaction on earlier occasions. True, she experiences intense pleasure and excitement, but nothing like the full ecstasy described on (*e.g.*) pp. 138–9 and 181; and her pleasure is submerged in successive waves of fright, reluctance, and shame. These emotions, in the circumstances, are surprising. 'She was a little startled and almost unwilling': why startled, after her earlier experiences with Mellors? And why, after her previous enjoyments of the 'sex thrill', unwilling? 'She . . . thought a woman would have died of shame'; what had she to be ashamed of? And then, in retrospect, 'How, in fear, she had hated it': what had she to be afraid of, or to hate?

Plainly, as Mr. Shonfield suggests, Lady Chatterley had on that night been subjected to some quite unusual treatment at Mellors' hands, and twenty pages later in the book we are given a clue as to what that treatment may have been. Immediately after the 'night of sensual passion' Lady Chatterley goes to stay in Venice, and while she is there she learns, by letters from her husband and his nurse, that Mellors' discarded wife, Bertha Coutts, has returned and is spreading slanderous rumours about him in the village. The nurse's letter gives mysterious hints (*L.C.*, p. 275): 'She goes about saying the most awful things about him, how he has women at the cottage, and how he behaved to her when they were married, the low, beastly things he did to her, and I don't know what all.' Her husband's letter was less equivocal. 'He is accused of all unspeakable things,' wrote Sir Clifford (*L.C.*, pp. 279–80), 'Of course there is really nothing in it. Humanity has always had a strange avidity for unusual sexual postures, and if a man likes to use his wife, as Benvenuto Cellini says, "in the Italian way", well that is a matter of taste.' That leaves us in no doubt about the nature of the accusation made by Bertha Coutts.[1]

It would be wrong, however, to regard the recriminations of a vindictive woman as affording a proof of what Mellors actually desired, or did; what she said might well be entirely the invention of malice.

But Lawrence has been careful to insert in his text a whole series of indications that Mellors did in fact suffer from an 'anal obsession,' as a recent contributor to *The Times Literary Supplement* (4 August 1961) described it: again and again, the keeper is represented as gloating over what Lawrence calls Lady Chatterley's 'haunches', her 'posteriors', or her 'buttocks', and Mellors himself, in his homelier jargon, her 'tail' or 'arse'.[2] I need (I hope) quote only one specimen (*L.C.*, p. 232): 'He watched the beautiful curving drop of her haunches. That fascinated him to-day. How it sloped with a rich down-slope to the heavy roundness of the buttocks! . . . He stroked her tail with his hand, long and subtly taking in the curves and the globe-fullness. "Tha's got such a nice tail on thee," he said, in

---

[1] The passages in Cellini's *Life* that Sir Clifford probably had in mind occur on pp. 292–3 of Bacci's edition (Florence, Sansoni, 1901): 'Insegniò loro che lei dicessi che io havessi usato seco al modo italiano; qual modo s'intendeva contro natura, cioè in soddomia'; and 'La Caterina disse, che io havevo usato seco al modo della Italia . . . ella vuol dire che tu hai usato seco fuora del vaso dove si fa figliuoli.' These passages are more easily accessible in J. A. Symonds' translation (Nimmo, 1885), Vol. II, pp. 206, 209.

[2] See, *e.g.*, *L.C.*, pp. 73, 180, 182, 229, 231, 232, 243, 245.

the throaty caressive dialect. "Tha's got the nicest arse of anybody. It's the nicest, nicest woman's arse as is!" '

But, it may be said, such appreciation, though outspoken, of these parts of the female body is no proof of perversion: many a sculptor has expressed just such feelings as Mellors' without incurring any suspicion of an ulterior sexual appetite. But Lawrence has hidden in this very passage the key to the nature of Mellors' anal interest: it is the openings concealed thereabouts in the female body that stimulate him: 'He laid his hand close and firm over her secret places, in a kind of close greeting' (*L.C.*, p. 233); and, again (*L.C.*, p. 232) 'He exquisitely stroked the rounded tail . . . and his finger-tips touched the two secret openings to her body, time after time, with a soft little brush of fire.' The 'secret places', the 'secret openings', these were what stirred in Mellors the sexual fire — and why? Lawrence gives us the answer in a single phrase (*L.C.*, p. 232): 'In between (the buttocks), folded in the secret warmth, the secret entrances!' By choosing the word 'entrance', and using it in the plural, Lawrence puts the nature of Mellors' sexual proclivities beyond the possibility of doubt.[1]

Yet a final question remains: the appetite was there in Mellors, but did he actually indulge it, during that 'night of sensual passion', on Lady Chatterley's person? And here one must observe that Lawrence throughout his extended description of that episode, is false to the rule that he follows so faithfully in every other 'sexual' passage in the book — the rule that prescribed a full and frank account of what occurred. Here, he relies on hints, suggestions, innuendoes, and simply does not tell the reader what actually happened. Yet here again he is careful to give us a clue so that in the end we shall be in no doubt about it. When Lady Chatterley, in Venice, hears what Bertha Coutts has been saying about the keeper, she is far from dismissing the accusations as a baseless slander; on the

---

[1] If there is any ambiguity about the kind of 'entering' envisaged, it is removed by Lady Chatterley herself: 'The phallus alone,' she reflected, 'could explore it' (*L.C.*, p. 259).

contrary, she knows well that they are true — and why?: 'Connie remembered the last night she had spent with him, and shivered. He had known all that sensuality, even with a Bertha Coutts!' (*L.C.*, p. 276). With this final link, identifying what she herself had experienced with what Bertha Coutts alleged, surely the chain of proof is complete and irrefragable?

'Connie remembered the last night she had spent with him, and shivered': Lawrence represents her first reaction to the news as 'a revulsion against the whole affair.' Indeed, one might have supposed that Lawrence's purpose in introducing this episode was to make plain his disapproval of the kind of sexual conduct it exemplifies, and to show how, as a result of the experience, Lady Chatterley was led to adopt a higher conception of sexual love. But that is not the case. Her revulsion was a passing mood, and it was brought on not by her experiences on that 'sensual' night but by the reflection that she had shared those experiences with a 'low' woman. The experience itself she treasured: 'I loved last night,' she had said, on the following morning, to her lover (*L.C.*, p. 262), and it was the memory of it (p. 277) that clinched her resolve to 'stick to him' and 'not go back on him.'

And Lawrence has told us that he agrees with her: sensuality, 'sheer sensuality', 'reckless, shameless sensuality', was for him an essential element in a full and 'valid' sexual relationship between man and woman: he must be a 'phallic huntsman' and she a 'physical slave'. It was in order to show the importance of this element in relations between the sexes that he gave the night of sensual passion its place in that 'steady progression' of sexual episodes to which the 'experts' bore witness at the trial.

More than this: Lawrence explicitly defended himself against the criticism that he knew he would provoke, and he did so in what is perhaps the best known and most frequently quoted passage in the book. He puts his defence into the mouth of one of his characters, Duncan Forbes; but there can be little doubt that Forbes is speaking for his creator: 'It comes', said Mr. Raymond Williams in his evidence at the trial (p. 134), 'through a particular character, and I would judge that it is very much Lawrence's own view.' This is the passage (it is quoted by the publishers on the back of the Penguin second edition):

'The more dirt you do on sex the better they like it. But if you believe in your own sex, and won't have it done dirt to, they'll down you. It's the one insane taboo left: sex as a natural and vital thing. They won't have it. You'll see, they'll hound that man down' (*L.C.*, p. 277).

It is not clear what is meant, in this context, by 'your own sex', by 'believing in it', or by the phrase 'do dirt to' (or 'on'). But the outburst is generally taken to be a vindication of the relationship of Lady Chatterley and Mellors against those who condemn it as unconventional because of the difference in their social standings, and as immoral because adulterous. Society — so the accepted interpretation runs — will 'down' those who flout social conventions in the name of love, and if you are open about your love and refuse either to conform or to conceal, you will be treated as outside the pale by 'respectable' people: don't be ashamed of loving a gamekeeper, if you really love him; don't be afraid to treat your marriage as annulled if it has ceased to be a true marriage; but do not expect the approval of society for such conduct.

Unfortunately the context does not permit this interpretation of the passage. For Lawrence takes care to make it plain to us that Forbes, so far from referring to such relationships as that of Mellors and Lady Chatterley, was actually unaware that any relationship between them existed. Lady Chatterley did not tell him anything about it: 'She didn't say she had been the keeper's lover, she only said she liked him' (*L.C.*, p. 276); on the other hand, she 'told Forbes the history of the man' — that is, she told him of the charges his wife was bringing against him, and it is to these, specifically, that Forbes must be referring in his tirade about society and sex. In order that there should be no doubt that this is what he is referring to, Lawrence makes

Forbes say it in so many words: 'You'll see, they'll hound that man down. And what's he done, after all? If he's made love to his wife all ends on, hasn't he a right to? She ought to be proud of it.' (*L.C.*, p. 277.) It is the relationship of Mellors with his own wife, Bertha Coutts, not his relationship with Lady Chatterley, that Forbes refers to. Love 'all ends on': that is what Forbes (and, if Mr. Raymond Williams is right, Lawrence) is talking about; 'she ought to be proud of it': that is his last word upon it.

'Granted that the case is proved,' a reader may at this point interpose, 'what purpose is served by this demonstration? What makes you want to expose an unpleasant element in a book which you confess that you yourself find distasteful?'

'A liking for honesty and a loathing of humbug' would be a true, and perhaps a sufficient, answer.

If a book is being widely read — and Penguin Books claim to have sold hundreds of thousands of copies of this production — it seems to me desirable that those who read it should be fully enlightened about its meaning. And this answer has all the more force in a case where the author is as important a literary figure as Lawrence, where the book constitutes (to use Mr. Gerald Gardiner's phrase) the 'crux of his work', and where the misunderstanding one is seeking to dispel directly concerns a significant element in his message.

But there is more to it than that. If the demonstration is sound, several interesting questions arise concerning the book and its author on the one hand and the trial and the 'expert' witnesses on the other.

The first of these questions was raised by Mr. Shonfield in ENCOUNTER, and had already been glanced at by the writer in the *Literary Supplement*. Lawrence was a passionate campaigner for openness and frankness in the treatment of sexual matters: 'the truth and the whole truth' — that was his creed — 'one should not be ashamed, or afraid, to tell it.' And *Lady Chatterley* was, supposedly, the book in which he put most fully into practice what he preached. This devotion to the cause of frankness, of directness, justified, according to the 'experts', his use in the book of the 'four-letter' words,[1] and it is certainly the justification he would himself have pleaded for the detailed descriptions of sexual intercourse that fill so many of its pages.

That being so, it is surely a remarkable fact that, at a climax of the book, Lawrence should (to use his own phrase) 'do dirt on' his own sexual creed, becoming covert and oblique instead of being open and direct, and relying on clues and suggestions instead of describing in plain and forthright language (as he does elsewhere in the book) what actually happened. Was he ashamed, or was he afraid? Either way (or, perhaps, both ways) he lost his nerve, so that in the very book in which he made his most violent protest against censorship he became (in Mr. Shonfield's phrase) his own censor; and in the very passage in which he utters his loudest pæan in praise of shamelessness ('She felt a triumph, almost a vainglory. . . . There was nothing left to disguise or be ashamed of'), shame seems to have overcome him.[2] This failure of integrity, this fundamental dis-

---

[1] It was asserted also by witnesses for the defence that Lawrence's purpose in using these words was to uplift them — to 'redeem' them, as one of them put it, or (to use counsel's word) to 'purify' them.

But in fact Lawrence's purpose, as he himself explained it, seems to have been the reverse. He loathed any attempt to 'spiritualise' love, to make it something that involved the whole personality; 'personal sympathy and personal love' led inevitably, he believed, to 'rage and hatred'. 'Complete intimacy' was 'a bore'. 'All that weary selfconsciousness between a man and a woman!', he makes Lady Chatterley herself exclaim, 'A disease!' (*L.C.*, p. 264); 'Marriage,' he said, 'is no marriage that is not basically and permanently phallic.' His purpose in using the 'taboo' words (as he called them) was to register (so to say) the earthy, physical, phallic nature of the kind of love he was contending for: 'If I use the taboo words,' he wrote (*A Propos of Lady Chatterley's Lover*, p. 60), 'there is a reason. We shall never free the phallic reality from the "uplift" taint till we give it its own phallic language, and use the obscene words. The greatest blasphemy of all against the phallic reality is this "lifting it to a higher plane".'

It is hardly necessary to say that none of the witnesses for the defence referred to this passage.

[2] Perhaps it is relevant to recall that the practice Lawrence was commending is (as I have explained above) a criminal offence, and Lawrence may have

honesty, not only is interesting as a human trait in Lawrence, but, as Mr. Shonfield suggests, may help to explain the failure of *Lady Chatterley's Lover* as a work of art. That is a question that deserves investigation by a seminar on Lawrence more thorough (if less expensive) than the 'expensive and thorough seminar' organized by Penguin Books at the Old Bailey.

Scarcely less puzzling is the question that arises concerning the Penguin 'seminar' itself. How many of the 'expert' witnesses, one wonders, can have understood the real meaning of Lawrence's account of the 'night of sensual passion'? It is hardly credible that students of Lawrence who had paid special attention to the book, and who put themselves forward as 'experts'[1] at the trial, should all of them have failed completely

thought that commendation of it would increase the likelihood of the book's being seized by the Customs or the police. This fear might be accepted as a reason for omitting the episode entirely, but it hardly explains his introducing it but not using plain terms. By doing that Lawrence surely laid himself open to the charge of wanting to 'have it both ways'.

[1] It is not clear, in several cases, in what their qualifications as experts consisted: 'I was brought up in a very literary family' was the basis (together with a classical scholarship at a girls' college) of one witness's claim to be a literary expert; another, a girl of twenty-one, had failed to get a First Class in English Literature, but had 'started to write a novel'.

Several were certainly not expert witnesses in the sense of being expert at giving evidence. Here is a specimen question and answer (*Trial*, p. 60): Q. 'How far, in your view, are the descriptions of sexual intercourse relevant or necessary to the theme or meaning of the book?' A. 'I think that Lawrence in this book was attempting to bring home to the imaginations of his readers certain aspects of modern society, the failure of relations between men and women, the degraded condition in which many people live.' The jury, no doubt, were duly impressed; but it will be seen that the answer bears not the slightest relation to the question asked.

Again, Mr. Gardiner asked a Prebendary (*Trial*, p. 89): 'Would it be more or less in accordance with Christian theology if some parts were replaced by asterisks?' The answer was: 'It would be less in accordance.' Neither counsel nor witness, surely, can have asked himself what theology had to do with the matter. And what is one to make of a religious 'expert' who in answer to the question, 'Has the word "phallic" always had a sacred connotation?' replies (*Trial*, p. 162): 'I don't know that it has *always* had a sacred connotation, but, like many words taken over from a pagan world, it has been baptised by Christians and made into a sacred word'?

to appreciate the meaning of this important episode in it.
Strange experts they must have been if that was so!

On the other hand, it is difficult to see how a witness who did
appreciate the veiled meaning of this passage could have given
an unqualified testimonial to Lawrence's outspokenness and
honesty in the description of sexual acts, or how such a witness
could have declared that there was nothing perverse or unnatural in Lawrence's attitude towards sex as revealed in the
book.

Yet witnesses for the defence repeatedly asserted that a
leading purpose of Lawrence in this novel was to vindicate, by
example, openness and frankness about sexual intercourse, and
not one of them suggested that at any point in it he was untrue
to this purpose. And as for the content of Lawrence's sexual
doctrine, as distinct from his frankness in describing sexual
acts, many of the experts testified to their approval of it in
terms which make it difficult to believe that they understood
what it was they were approving. A Bishop, for instance, maintained (*Trial*, p. 71) that Lawrence represented the sexual act
'as in a real sense something sacred,[1] as in a real sense an act of
holy communion'; one Professor declared roundly (*Trial*, p.
147) that his descriptions of sexual intercourse were 'never
sadistic or perverted', and another (*Trial*, p. 76) that they were
'absolutely necessary, to show that a union of human beings
must be based on an adequate kind of sexual intercourse —
sexual intercourse which was, in his own words, "valid and
precious" '; and a woman editor expressed the view (*Trial*, p.
157) that Lawrence associated sex 'with tenderness, with
thought for the other person, with the creation of new life . . .
not with violence or cruelty or perversion'. Even Mr. Gardiner,
in opening his case (*Trial*, p. 34), stated explicitly and without
qualification that the book was 'a book in which there is no

---

[1] 'Sacred' was a word repeatedly used in this connexion by the witnesses:
'You may think it is significant,' said Mr. Gardiner in his closing speech, 'that
the word "sacred" should, quite independently and in a different context, have
been used by so many of these witnesses' (*Trial*, p. 186).

kind of perversion at all'. Such language is, to say the least,
difficult to reconcile with an understanding of Lawrence's
descriptions of the 'phallic hunting out' and his praise of love
'all ends on'.

Particularly intriguing in this respect is the evidence of Sir
William Emrys Williams, who appeared in the witness-box in a
dual capacity, both as a literary expert who had read all
Lawrence's works[1] and as a director of the defendant company.
When he was asked about the significance of the 'purple'
passages, Sir William replied that 'the whole point that
(Lawrence) was determined to impress upon us was that love
can be a failure, love can be dirty, love can be clean; and these
two people go through the whole cycle until they do discover
the wholesome fulfilment' (*Trial*, p. 88). As for the 'four-letter'
words, Sir William thought that to substitute asterisks for
them 'would make the thing just a dirty book': Lawrence (he
said) 'wants them in full. He wants no shorthand, he wants no
disguise, he wants no concealment' (*Trial*, p. 89). I would cast
no doubt on the sincerity of these answers, or their appropriate-
ness to the questions actually asked; but it is not easy to deduce
from them how Sir William, if he had been confronted by
counsel with the relevant passages, would have explained the

[1] Asked whether Penguin Books proposed to publish the whole of Lawrence's
works, Sir William replied (*Trial*, p. 86): 'Not quite the whole. There are two
or three which we shall, I think, not publish, such as the *Psycho-analysis of the
Unconscious*, simply because it is virtually an unreadable book.' Lawrence in
fact wrote no book called *The Psycho-analysis of the Unconscious*. Perhaps Sir
William conflated in his mind two books — he may have found them both
unreadable — *Fantasia of the Unconscious* and *Psycho-analysis and the
Unconscious*, neither of which is included in the Penguin series of Lawrence's
works.

Some will regret the decision to exclude them: 'If the millions of people who
read *Lady Chatterley's Lover* would only read his *Psycho-analysis and the
Unconscious* and his *Fantasia of the Unconscious*', writes Sir Herbert Read in
Does Pornography Matter? (Routledge & Kegan Paul, 1961), 'there might be
some hope of a change of mind and heart that would lead eventually to a new
way of education, a new structure of society, and an end to sexual perversion
and pornography.' From the business point of view, however, *Lady Chatterley*
was no doubt a better proposition.

'night of sensual passion' ('the wholesome fulfilment'?) and
Lawrence's treatment of it ('no disguise, no concealment'?),
and the subsequent vindication of what it really stood for by
Forbes — 'She ought to be proud of it' — and by Lady Chatterley herself.

And that leads to the final, and not the least intriguing,
question: if the full truth had been made clear and brought
home to the witnesses and to the jury, would the verdict in the
case have been a different one? Perhaps it is significant in this
connexion that defending counsel — though, in the words of
Mr. Gardiner (*Trial*, p. 37), 'Every part of the book (was)
relevant to the defence' — did not put this passage to their
witnesses or refer to it in addressing the jury. Is it fantastic to
detect an anxiety on the part of Mr. Jeremy Hutchinson, when
examining Mr. Raymond Williams (*Trial*, p. 134), to steer him
away from the fatal passage? Did he fear that the witness
really understood its meaning and might be going to explain it
to the jury? Again, when Mr. Griffith Jones launched out on a
quotation from the passage in his closing speech, Mr. Gardiner
objected: it had not (he said) been put to any of the witnesses.
The Judge over-ruled the objection and then Mr. Griffith Jones
let it go, with 'I don't know what it means' (*Trial*, p. 223). Did
the defence at this point breathe a sigh of heartfelt satisfaction?[1]

What would have been the effect upon the jury of a complete
exposition of the truth, one can but speculate. But Mr. C. H.
Rolph, the editor of the Penguin summary of the trial, gives us
a pointer, based on his own observation of the proceedings:
even the unexplained innuendo contained in Mr. Griffith
Jones's 'not very easy to know what he is driving at', was

[1] Still more effective use of these passages might have been made by the
prosecution if the book (like *The Ladies' Directory* in the case *Regina* v. *Shaw*)
had been made the subject of a charge under the Common Law of conspiracy
to commit a public mischief (as, in theory, it seems that it still might be). It
would then have been enough, in order to secure a conviction, to prove that it
affronted public decency, without showing that it tended to corrupt its readers.

enough, it seems, to have 'visibly shocked some members of the jury' (*Trial*, p. 221), and a similar vague hint a little later evokes from Mr. Rolph the comment, 'Again the innuendo, again the shock.'

If the prosecution had brought home to the Court Lawrence's commendation of something that — to quote his own words (*L.C.*, p. 258) — 'was not really love. It was not voluptuousness. It was sensuality . . . reckless shameless sensuality', the shock to the jury might have been greater, and if the passages in which he described it had been put squarely to the witnesses who praised him at such length for the 'sacredness' and 'spirituality' that he abhorred, the verdict might have been a different one. It may well be that the policy of silence on this crucial point saved the day for the defence.

Afterthoughts on
Regina v. Penguin Books Ltd.

*

The nine minutes' wonder created by my article on the *Lady Chatterley* case has now subsided, and I myself no longer feel the desire to answer, one by one, the critics — angry, satirical, or merely contemptuous — who attacked it. None the less, I should like to set down a few afterthoughts about the controversy, and to remove, if I can, one or two misunderstandings on which some of the critics seem to have based their strictures.

Two strains predominated in the loud chorus of dispraise: there were those who said that the interpretation that I put upon the disputed passage in the book was so obviously right that everyone had always accepted it, and that therefore my article was otiose; and there were those who insisted that I had not proved my case, some of them putting forward an alternative, 'innocent', interpretation as being possibly, or even certainly, correct.

The first semi-chorus was the louder, if not the larger, of the two; and, as the force of my demonstration made itself felt among readers, it recruited a number of deserters from the second — people who at first protested against the suggestion that my interpretation could be right, and then persuaded themselves that they had accepted it 'all along'. But there are still many people who question my reading of the passage, or positively support an alternative explanation. They include several of the 'experts' who gave evidence in favour of the book, counsel (I believe) for the defence, and a number of those who wrote letters on the subject to ENCOUNTER (and to the *Spectator*), one of whom claimed that an explanation different from mine has 'long been accepted by most "normal" men and women'. The existence of this considerable body of opinion seems in itself to be a sufficient answer to the first school of critics: an interpretation that was (and still is) so strongly challenged cannot be said to have been so obviously right as not to stand in need of demonstration.

That my article did demonstrate its correctness I have no doubt. I can only refer those who question this to the argument leading up to my conclusion; not one of the critics who disputed that conclusion has even attempted to pick a hole in the *nexus* of reasoning by which it was reached. The clues planted by Lawrence in the text point unequivocally to one interpretation, and though he did not make his meaning obvious, he must have intended serious readers so to understand it.

A weightier criticism came from others: 'Granted,' they said, 'that you proved your thesis; granted that Lawrence did not make his meaning plain; still, your article was superfluous because it concerned a question of no importance. What does it matter exactly what happened on the "night of sensual passion"? It is absurd — indeed, it is deplorable — to focus attention on such physical details.'

I cannot help thinking that many of those who took this line were influenced more deeply than they would have cared to admit — more deeply, perhaps, than they themselves recognized — by the nature of the question at issue. What they really meant, I suspect, was not 'The question is an unimportant one, and therefore it was not worth your while to raise it,' but 'The question is an unpleasant one, and therefore we should be much more comfortable if you had left it alone'.[1]

I sympathize with this reluctance to approach the matter, but I do not think that one should yield to it: those who care

---

[1] I suspect also that many who challenged the correctness of my interpretation were, likewise, swayed less by reason than by a natural reluctance to admit the truth of a theory that they found repugnant.

Afterthoughts on Regina v. Penguin Books Ltd.

for literature and value truth ought not to shirk discussion of an important question, or to minimize its importance, simply because they find it 'difficult' or unpleasant.

Still, the criticism, whatever actuated it, demands an answer. Was the question, after all, important enough to justify its being made the subject of an inquiry that shocked the feelings of many decent people?

That the 'night of sensual passion' is an important episode in the novel can hardly be denied. Those witnesses were right who insisted at the trial that each of the 'sexual encounters' was inserted by Lawrence with a special purpose, and this particular one occupies a crucial place both in the account of the heroine's relations with her lover and in the development of the main theme in the book — her gradually increasing awareness of the full meaning and possibilities of sex. Lawrence makes this clear both by his description of her feelings during that 'sensual' night and by his account of her subsequent recollections of it. Plainly the episode, however it is to be interpreted, is of prime importance in the book.

But how much does it matter what the true interpretation of it is? This is never a simple question when asked about something in a work of fiction. The query may have an aesthetic intention: How much does our appreciation of the passage depend upon our understanding precisely what the author meant by it? Or, if the work has a 'message', it may mean 'How far does our understanding of the author's general intention depend upon our interpreting this feature of it correctly?' And, if the message is a controversial one, the question may have a practical significance: How far — it may mean — would our opinion (or the general opinion) of the author himself be affected by a new light thrown upon the meaning of what he wrote?[1]

---

[1] It is instructive to consider, in the light of the above, the importance of ascertaining the correct answer to the following questions: Was Hamlet 'really' mad? Was Hamlet dark or fair? Were some of the sonnets in which Shakespeare expressed intense physical passion addressed to a young man?

Afterthoughts on Regina v. Penguin Books Ltd.

In the present case it is impossible to keep these questions wholly separate. *Lady Chatterley's Lover* is something more than a novel. It is, in large part, a series of poetical passages describing, or attempting to convey in words, the sensations accompanying the sexual act. It is also a tract, in which Lawrence (as his letters show) intended to convey, more frankly than he had ever done before, his most mature views upon the subject of sex. These elements in the book do not (I think) hold together, and Lawrence's failure to make them coalesce in a way that satisfies the reader is (or so it seems to me) one of the reasons, but not the only one, for the failure of the book as a work of art. Yet these elements cannot be judged apart from each other: both the poetry and the story are intended to illustrate and to bring home to the reader the validity of Lawrence's sexual doctrine.

One of the principal theses in Lawrence's doctrine is the necessity, in a completely 'valid' sexual relationship between a man and a woman, of two elements: 'tenderness' on the one hand and on the other a 'fiery', cruel, sensuality that demands on the part of the woman complete submission and an entire absence of sexual shame. Lawrence described the 'night of sensual passion', and gave it a climactic position both in his story and in the development of his theme, in order to bring home to his readers the importance of the second of these two elements. And this the episode fails to do unless it is understood as Lawrence intended it to be. He is deliberately and definitely challenging convention on this point, and the challenge fails to 'register' if the episode is given an 'innocent' explanation — if it is assumed that nothing 'unnatural' was intended — that it is merely a trivial question of a variation of posture.

If we are to judge the importance of a right understanding of the episode by reference to the author's intention, we can only say that Lawrence would have scornfully rejected the well-meant efforts of his present-day defenders to play down its significance or to provide him with an 'innocent' explanation of it.

Of course the full value of a piece of poetical writing, whether in prose or verse, often does not depend at all upon a precise realization of what it describes; indeed, a too precise realization may ruin its effectiveness. Of nothing is this truer than the description of physical passion, which is best conveyed not by giving details, nor by 'leaving them to the imagination', but by so satisfying the imagination that it does not ask for them — '*Non è lecito*,' says the narrator, at just such a point in Giuseppe di Lampedusa's *Lighea*, '*non sarebbe d'altronde pietoso verso di te, entrare in particolari. . . . Ripensa a quanto Balzac non ha osato esprimere nella "Passion dans le désert"*.' Balzac's silence at the climax of his superb story was not (as '*osato*' suggests) due to a failure of nerve; it was simply that his art was so delicate that he did not need to say more. Lawrence, who was trying to combine a poem with a tract, evidently felt the need, for the tract's sake, to make his meaning precise, and yet could not bring himself to be unambiguous. Hence (in Mr. Shonfield's words) the 'strident ejaculatory writing' at this point, 'which is of outstanding badness even among the long passages of girl's gush writing that the book contains.' It is not that Lawrence does not say enough; he says too much, and yet, as Mr. Shonfield concludes, 'he manages to mask and muff, if not to conceal entirely, his essential message.'[1]

Other writers confirm my estimate of the importance attached by Lawrence to this particular perversion as an element in a full sexual relationship between a man and a woman.

In an article 'Lawrence, Joyce, and Powys' in *Essays in*

[1] Of course it was not my intention to suggest that Lawrence ought here, in order to make his meaning plain, to have descended to crude or clinical details. In so far as my language suggested that he did so elsewhere in the novel, the point made by Mr. David Sylvester in his letter to ENCOUNTER was a good one. But it remains true that Lawrence's boasted 'frankness' broke down at this point.

Afterthoughts on *Regina v. Penguin Books Ltd.*

Criticism, October 1961 (which I did not see until my own essay was in proof) Professor G. Wilson Knight maintains that the 'night of sensual passion' provides the fullest evidence of an obsession on Lawrence's part to which several of his poems also bear witness; he traces the development of this obsession through *Women in Love* and to a climax in *Lady Chatterley*, and seeks to illumine it by a *pot pourri* of references to the 'posterior locations' (as he calls them) drawn from the unbridled sexual fantasies of *Ulysses*. The passages that Professor Knight quotes from Joyce will not, I think, bear the weight he seeks to put upon them; nor, it seems to me, do his quotations from J. C. Powys help to elucidate the dark places in Lawrence.[1] But what does emerge from his curious gallimaufry is the importance of the part played in Lawrence's 'sexual ethic' by this particular kind of perversion.

The importance of this feature in Lawrence's 'ethic' is also asserted, more concisely and more authoritatively, by Eliseo Vivas in *D. H. Lawrence: the failure and triumph of art* (Allen & Unwin, November, 1961). In his chapter on *Lady Chatterley's Lover*, Professor Vivas says that the references to 'the Italian way' reveal the 'love-ethic' of Lawrence, and that they indicate 'practices that Lawrence and his admirers agree are essential to burn out the "deepest, oldest shames, in the most secret places" '. 'Not only have those critics who admire Lawrence's love-ethic ignored or overlooked all that it involves,' says Professor Vivas, 'but they have not observed how radical is the transvaluation of values that he advocates.' To this 'radical

---

[1] Professor Knight's invocation of one author to explain another seems to me unhelpful — as when, for instance, he says that a reference to 'animality' in Joyce 'lends point' to Lawrence's 'phallic hunting-out' in *Lady Chatterley*, and adds that 'Joyce's concentrations may be compared with the back view of a man's agonizingly beautiful body in *Women in Love* and with the yet greater insistence on the arsenerastic, replacing vague terms such as "loins" with a more precise terminology, throughout *Lady Chatterley's Lover*'. What meaning — or indeed what derivation — the Professor attributes to his word 'arsenerastic' is not made clear by the dozen page-references to the novel appended by him at this point.

transvaluation' the right interpretation of the crucial passage provides a necessary key.

Several critics were made very angry by my suggestion that a true understanding of the passage was of practical as well as intrinsic importance. I ventured to say that if its meaning had been put squarely to those of the experts at the trial who had not really understood it — clergymen, professors and lecturers in literature, heads of schools and colleges — and if its significance had thus been brought home to the jury, it might have affected the judgment that both witnesses and jury passed upon the work. I still think that this is true, and I suspect that the critics were angry not because they were convinced that I was wrong in stating this opinion, but because they were afraid that I was right.

I did not impute deliberate bad faith to the witnesses or any sort of impropriety to counsel; and this was not out of caution, but because I sincerely believed in their honesty. But I felt (and I still feel) that many of the witnesses, in their anxiety to vindicate their own high-mindedness and broad-mindedness, and in their eagerness to strike a blow for liberty and literature, allowed themselves to give a false account of Lawrence's sexual ethic as revealed in *Lady Chatterley's Lover*,[1] and that the trial was in consequence largely a display of shadow-boxing and the verdict something of a mockery. And, looking back on it, I sympathize less with the *bien pensant* progressives, who were indignant at not being allowed to get away unchallenged with a questionable victory, than with the correspondent who said in

---

[1] In particular, some of the witnesses grossly misinterpreted Mellors' panegyric of 'chastity' and his attack on 'wearisome philandering' in the closing paragraphs of the book. Chastity, for Mellors, was simply 'the peace that comes of' copulation (he used a shorter word), and by 'philandering' he did not mean going from one woman to another for sexual satisfaction — that had been his own practice, as his heartless recital of his amours (*L.C.*, pp. 208–12) reveals — he meant making love without 'sex'. Here, and on p. 264, Lawrence's characters are a mouthpiece for his own doctrine: 'Love is chiefly bunk; an over-exaggeration of the spiritual and individualistic and analytic side'; he was preoccupied with what Dr. Leavis has called 'human mating'.

ENCOUNTER that it would have been 'cleaner and saner in the long run' to let the novel be judged for what it was.

In pointing out the unsatisfactory features of the trial I was not intending, of course, to suggest that the case should be retried. No one knew better than I that that was out of the question, and I should have deplored, even if it had been legally possible, any attempt to re-open the matter judicially. Indeed, though I think that the verdict might very probably have been a different one had the true meaning of the passage been brought home to the jury, I am very doubtful whether they *ought* to have been so affected by it; that is a different question, and a more difficult one to answer. I should myself be inclined to agree with the correspondent who said in ENCOUNTER that Lawrence's account of the 'night of sensual passion' was not likely to encourage his readers, if they understood it, to indulge in the practice it describes, and that therefore the possibility of its being correctly interpreted did not increase the likelihood of the book's 'corrupting' its readers.[1]

What I have so far said leaves unanswered what to many will seem the most important question concerning the trial: was the verdict on the book taken as a whole a right one? Much of the critics' rancour was due, I think, to the belief that my article constituted an attack on the verdict that vindicated *Lady Chatterley's Lover* and on the Act that, in effect, legalized its publication. One correspondent challenged me to say whether I deplored the verdict, and another suggested that in not stating my own views on censorship I was myself guilty of the evasiveness that I imputed to Lawrence.

My main reason for not declaring my views on these questions was that the rightness or wrongness of the verdict was irrelevant

[1] If the book had been tried (like *The Ladies' Directory*) under the common law as well as (or instead of) under the Act of 1959, I should say that the true meaning of the passage was so veiled that its latent significance did not constitute an affront to decency — if indeed such an affront (as was suggested in *Regina* v. *Shaw*) can amount to a public mischief.

to the point I was seeking to make, and still less relevant was my own opinion on the wider questions concerning censorship and morals that lay on or beneath the surface of the case. Nor had I any decided opinion upon these questions to declare. They seem to me to be very difficult to answer; and the fact that ENCOUNTER's correspondents, and most of the witnesses at the trial, found them easy, does nothing to decrease my own uncertainty about them — for the answers that they so confidently advanced were full of contradictions. Some of them were opposed to any censorship at all; others, including several of the witnesses who spoke out most loudly against the suppression of *Lady Chatterley*, were clear that 'pornography' should be suppressed by law. But why pornography should be suppressed, how it should be defined, and how in a given case it should be decided whether a work is pornographic — on these questions the critics were quite unable to agree.

I am not myself so confident as they: all I can say is that if there is to be a law imposing censorship, the Jenkins Act seems to me to be not a bad one, and an improvement on the law as it stood before its passing. But I am inclined to think that the real, if unconscious, motive behind public approval of the censor's activities is a feeling that the law ought not to permit the general distribution of what is generally thought to be outrageously indecent, and it seems to me that this affords a sounder basis for censorship than a desire that the law should protect public morals in this field. Since, however, the Act of 1959 is not concerned with public decency, the possible application of such a doctrine to *Lady Chatterley's Lover* was not before the Court.

How I should have voted if I had been on the jury at the Old Bailey I do not know. But I may say that I found much that was ridiculous and (in various ways) repugnant to me both in the book and in the evidence given on its behalf; that I do not think it is of great value as a work of literature, or that it is necessary to have read it in order to appreciate the body of work that Lawrence produced before he wrote it; and that it seems to me from every point of view a pity that Penguin Books should have launched it on the public at three shillings and sixpence a copy.

The debate was raised to a higher level by the most eloquent and the most sympathetic of my critics, Mr. Colin MacInnes. Sympathetic, not because he sympathized with me — far from it! — but because I found in his protests much with which I myself could sympathize. Mr. MacInnes wrote with a passionate concern to vindicate freedom in life and art against the distortions of puritanism and the dead hand of the law. He excoriated the Old Bailey witnesses, in language far more scathing than any used by me, not for what they said, or failed to say, in evidence, but for taking any part at all in what he called 'the hateful trial'. They 'dishonoured Lawrence', in his view, as much by their defence of him as did the prosecution by its attack. The verdict, so far from being the victory claimed by Penguin Books for light over darkness, did much more harm than good, for it meant that, instead of hundreds, millions would thenceforth buy the novel as a 'dirty book'. As for my article, by drawing attention to 'an irrelevance' it increased the book's attraction for the prurient and provided another stone for the Puritans to throw at Lawrence's reputation.

Mr. MacInnes accepted my interpretation of the disputed passage — but what (he asked, in effect) does it matter how it is interpreted? And what does it matter whether the verdict would have been affected by a fuller understanding of it? Of what importance was the verdict, anyhow? Art, or at least great Art, should be outside the range of the law, and 'laws seeking to govern literary truth [whatever that may mean] are totally to be mistrusted'. The Act of 1959, so far from having improved the law by allowing artistic merit, at least in some cases, to save a work from suppression, was a step in the wrong direction because it brought within the range of the law something that properly lay outside it.

Of course, behind all this, muddled though it is, there is a feeling with which one cannot fail to sympathise. It goes against the grain to take a line that may seem to mark one as unfriendly to the Arts or to the liberty of the individual. And I suspect that the Arts — though I do not care to rave about them in print — mean as much to me as they do to Mr. MacInnes, and that my views on sexual morality differ far less from his than he supposes. But his enthusiasm betrays him into a number of judgments that seem to me disputable or plainly indefensible. So far as they directly concern Lawrence and his work, I shall not attempt to answer them — indeed, it would be waste of time for me to do so: 'Who cares,' asks Mr. MacInnes, 'if dons, barristers, and pedants make idiots of themselves when they speak and write of art? That is what they are for.' This neatly lists my own disqualifications, and I will not offer opinions that have been discounted in advance as idiotic. But Mr. MacInnes must surely recognize that the general position from which he chooses to launch his attack upon my article cannot be rationally defended. He claims that Art, or 'great' Art, or Art produced by writers 'of the quality of' Lawrence or writers with 'Lawrence's gifts and intentions', should be above the law. But someone must determine whether a challenged work is 'Art' or 'great Art', or Art 'of the quality' that entitles it to exemption — and to whom is that function to be entrusted?

Art is in a sense, it is true, above and beyond the law; no Act of Parliament can (in Mr. MacInnes' phrase) 'govern literary truth' or control the artistic imagination. But artists live in the same world as ordinary men, and the artist cannot claim exemption from the laws that regulate society. Those who care for Art and feel for the artist, and want to improve his position under the law, will probably in the long run help him better by facing the facts involved in claims made on his behalf than by evading or concealing those of them that seem 'unpleasant', like so many of the witnesses in the present case, or by attempting, like Mr. MacInnes, to 'contract out' completely.[1]

[1] I have left for a footnote the unkindest criticism of all: several correspondents declared that my article showed that its author was entirely lacking in a

sense of humour. To this charge — though none more wounding can be brought against an Englishman — I can only enter a plea of guilty; indeed, it is a charge on which I could hardly hope to be acquitted, seeing that two of our most successful professional humorists are among my critics. But there is nothing that, at my age, I can do about this; and when I confess that, reading Mr. Osbert Lancaster's epigram — so obviously humorous in its intention — I was unable to raise a smile, and that I suffered no such incapacity as I perused the solemn protestations of Mr. Stephen Potter, I shall only be taken, I am afraid, to have given a fresh proof of my unfortunate inability to distinguish between what is ridiculous and what is not.

The Housman Dilemma[1]

*

'And my executor shall destroy without exception all my unpublished MSS.' — that well-worn testamentary injunction
raises an issue as old as the *Aeneid*, and the considerations on
either side — the sacredness of a dying author's wishes, as
against the duty to literature, to posterity — are familiar and
nicely balanced. On the death of A. E. Housman the old problem arose in a new and complicated form. The story is a tangled
one, and it may be worth while to set it out in some detail.

Housman's brother Laurence was, by his will, permitted 'to
select from my verse manuscript writing and to publish any
poems which appear to him to be completed and to be not
inferior in quality to the average of my published poems', and
directed 'to destroy all other poems and fragments of verse'.
Mr. Laurence Housman made, and published, his selection
from the four poetical note-books left by A.E.H., and then, as
the will directed, destroyed all leaves that contained nothing
but unpublished matter. There remained a number of leaves
carrying on one side drafts (in varying stages of finish) of published poems, and on the other side jottings and fragmentary
drafts of poems which A.E.H. did not publish and which his
brother decided were not worthy of publication. He was anxious
to preserve the first, but felt himself in duty bound to destroy
the second.

In this situation, Mr. Laurence Housman should surely have
made up his mind one way or the other. If he held his brother's
wishes paramount, he should have destroyed all unpublished
fragments, even if that involved sacrificing in the process drafts

[1] A review of *The Manuscript Poems of A. E. Housman*. Edited by Tom
Burns Haber, 1955.

71

of published poems. If, on the other hand, he thought that the interests of literature required that those wishes should be disregarded, he should have preserved everything. Had he taken the second course he would have had his critics; but, right or wrong, he could have looked them squarely in the face.

Instead, Mr. Housman pursued a middle course. From the ambiguous leaves he cut away such portions as bore on both sides unpublished matter: and then, erasing or overscoring in ink or pencil everything, or almost everything, that had not already seen print, he pasted the remaining leaves and parts of leaves on to folio sheets so as to expose to view only the texts of poems which A.E.H., or he himself, had published.

In this unsatisfactory condition the manuscripts were sold to an American purchaser, the right to publish any still unpublished material being reserved to the author's estate. Nothing had been done to remove this restriction when the manuscripts passed by gift to the Library of Congress in 1940. In 1945 the Library authorities removed the leaves from the sheets on which they were pasted, and remounted them with hinges, so that the erased and cancelled texts on the versos were again exposed to view. This was done not with a view to publication but solely in order the better to preserve the manuscripts, on which the adhesive material was said to be having a deleterious effect. It was in 1947 that Mr. Tom Burns Haber, of Ohio State University, began to interest himself in the material thus made accessible, and during the summers of 1950, 1951 and 1952 he set to work deciphering what Mr. Laurence Housman had taken such pains to hide, and announced his intention of publishing his results. At this stage, protests were made in *The Times Literary Supplement* about Mr. Haber's project. Was it possible to stop the publication of the unpublished jottings and fragments by legal action? If so, who had the right to stop it? And — legal objections apart — was it, morally, right so to disregard the wishes of the poet and frustrate the evident intentions of his brother, through whom the manuscripts had been acquired?

It appears that, if objection had been taken and persisted in, it would have been possible to stop the publication by action in the Courts; for Mr. Haber, writing in answer to his critics in the *Literary Supplement* on 7 November 1952, declared, 'All legal objections to this project have now been withdrawn'; and he says again, in his preface to the present book: 'All legal objections have been withdrawn, in writing, by Laurence Housman and Barclay's Bank, the designated trustees.' Exactly how this withdrawal of objection was secured, Mr. Haber does not tell us; nor does he tell anything of Mr. Laurence Housman's attitude in the matter at any stage. Mr. Housman himself, however, has left the public in no doubt about his feelings; writing to the *Oxford Mail* on 3 March 1955, he says:

'I made the great mistake of thinking that any manuscripts lodged at the Library of Congress would be treated with the same respect as those which I also lodged at the British Museum; and for that reason I failed to take the commercial precaution of securing the copyright. Had I done so none of these deplorable quotations could have been published.'

These remarks are in more than one respect misleading: Mr. Housman did not 'lodge' the manuscripts in the Library of Congress, and no step on his part was necessary in order to 'secure' a copyright which was already his — and which, it seems, he must at some stage have surrendered to the Library or to Mr. Haber. However this may be, it seems clear that if he surrendered his rights, Mr. Housman regretted having done so: and it seems equally clear that Mr. Haber was aware of this in November 1952. By then, however, it was too late for Mr. Housman to retract, and Mr. Haber evidently intended to show him no mercy: for after announcing, in the letter already quoted, that legal objections had been withdrawn, he continued as follows:

'There remains the ethical objection. This received its final answer when the persons standing nearest to the documents decided to preserve them and negotiated their sale. This was a sane and sensible decision, at which few will cavil. *Nescit vox missa reverti.*'

After this unkindly taunt, he observed somewhat cryptically:

'Finally it is to be hoped that those who knowingly risked censure in handling the manuscript as they did will not at this late date shrink from the consequences of their choice; certainly they need not join in the chorus of dissent. Their decision was as right as it is irrevocable.'

It looks as if the Library authorities had expressed misgivings which Mr. Haber was anxious to allay. If so, he was, it seems, successful; for the present opinion of the Library, he assures us in his preface to this volume, is that the publication 'involves no ethical consideration which might "embarrass the strictest sense of scholarly propriety".'

We will leave it to the common reader to form his own conclusions about the 'scholarly propriety' of these proceedings and to pass judgment as he thinks fit on the actors in the sorry drama, adding only that Mr. Haber says no word about this part of the story in the otherwise very full 'History' of the manuscripts which forms Part One of the book under review.

'Otherwise very full': but there is one remarkable omission. In quoting the all-important clause in Housman's will — 'And I permit him but do not enjoin him to select from my verse manuscript writing and to publish any poems which appear to him to be completed and to be not inferior in quality to the average of my published poems, *and I direct him to destroy all other poems and fragments of verse*' — Mr. Haber omits, and omits only, the words we have italicized. He quotes in full the order (though it is not strictly relevant to his purpose) to destroy all *prose* manuscripts, and it is to this that a reader might well think he is referring on the single occasion when he mentions an 'order for destruction'; but nowhere in his book is the crucial direction of the testator to destroy unpublished poetical texts quoted or even paraphrased. Readers can draw

their own conclusions about the reason for this strange
omission.

Candour is the first quality of a true scholar; and surely Mr.
Haber would have done better to say explicitly that A. E.
Housman had prohibited, and (if such was the fact) that his
brother deplored, what had been, and was being, done, but that
the editor was undertaking his tasks in the interests of poetry
and criticism.

Is poetry, or is criticism, in fact the richer for the publication
of this matter? Housman's reputation, probably, will neither
gain nor lose by what is now revealed. Here and there is a line
or two of characteristic and not unworthy poetry:

> *Haste for the heaven is westered since you came:*
> *Day falls, night climbs, the hour has lost its name;*
> *Quick, quick! the lightning's pace were weary, slow,*
> *And here you loiter spelling gravestones: go.*

and, in a less familiar vein:

> *Some air that swept the Arabian strand*
> *When the great gulf was calm,*
> *Some wind that waved in morning land*
> *The plumage of the palm.*

But most of the jottings are no more than chips from the
author's workshop, stamped with his character, and sometimes
even reading like parodies of his style. Many, no doubt, are
transcripts of those *vers donnés* that came into his head, as he
explained in *The Name and Nature of Poetry*, without any
conscious effort of composition on his part. No one will judge
him by them, for better or for worse. But his admirers, and not
only they, will be interested to observe how often a solitary line
or stanza, years after its first transcription, was worked into a
poem so perfectly that no reader of the completed whole would
suspect its independent origin.

More interesting than fragments of abortive poems are the

abandoned variants in the text of poems familiar in *A Shropshire Lad* and *Last Poems*, revealing as they do the poet's first and second, even his fifth and sixth, thoughts, his touchings and retouchings, his repeated refining of his gold. One stanza of the last piece in *A Shropshire Lad* he had to rewrite (he tells us in *The Name and Nature*) thirteen times; the manuscript of that particular piece is not preserved, but the notebooks afford plenty of analogous examples. The changes seem to have been almost always for the better and the comparison is always of interest. It is a pity that Mr. Haber has given only a small selection of the variants in the text of published poems; the temptation to call his book *The Manuscript Poems of A. E. Housman* — a misleading hardly, indeed, an accurate, title — and the desire to present 'Eight Hundred Lines of Hitherto Uncollected Verse' was no doubt too strong for him. His book therefore in the main consists of a mass of what he correctly describes as 'workshop material' which has not yet, in any form, been exposed to the public view.

The presentation of this material is a work which, if it was worth doing, was worth doing well. Indeed, work of this kind, above all others, needs to be done scrupulously well if it is to be done at all. What are the attributes that are needed for the task? They are not many and not rare ones: patience to disentangle and rearrange the material; an eye capable of reading so much of the text as is decipherable; accuracy in transcribing it where it is clear; a becoming humility, where it is doubtful; and an ear so attuned to the poet's voice that it can tell, where the eye is defeated, what he must, or might, or could not possibly, have written. Perhaps it is not unreasonable also to ask that an editor of Housman should be capable of understanding Latin and of writing English.

Of these attributes Mr. Haber has none, in any adequate degree, except the first. He has patiently reconstructed out of the materials before him as much as remains of A.E.H.'s four poetical notebooks; but he is sadly deficient in the power of

seeing what his author wrote and of transcribing accurately
what he sees: he lacks the intellectual humility that confesses
the doubtfulness of a doubtful reading; and he is patently deaf
to the tones of Housman's voice.

Three or four stanzas will afford at once a further indication
of the poetical quality of the material with which Mr. Haber is
dealing, and of his competence to deal with it. On page 33 of his
book Mr. Haber prints the following quatrain, written in manuscript, 'in pencil, beneath wavy cancellation in pencil':

> *As often under sighing oak*
> *drowsing*
> *Or near musing hidden laid*
> *Maiden and youth in whispers spoke,*
> *In whispers, youth and maid.*

'If there are reasonable grounds for conjecture in the reading of
an erased or cancelled section,' says Mr. Haber, 'my reading is
given, followed by an interrogation sign and enclosed in
brackets.' Can it really be that Mr. Haber did not think that
'hidden', which makes nonsense of line 2, was a sufficiently
doubtful reading to deserve an 'interrogation sign'? Would not
three minutes' thought have suggested to him that 'linden'
(under sighing oak — near musing linden) was more probably
the right reading? But 'thought' as Housman himself once
observed, 'is irksome, and three minutes is a long time'; neither
his eye nor his ear suggested to Mr. Haber that anything was
wrong with 'hidden', and he prints it without any sign of misgiving.

On the next page Mr. Haber prints the couplet ('faded ink,
beneath wavy cancellation in ink'):

> *Never, or ever, shine or snow,*
> *That son of God I used to know.*

Did it not occur to Mr. Haber, on grounds of sense and sound,
that Housman must, or (to say the least) might, have written

not 'or ever' but 'o never'? Or can it be that what is hidden by the 'wavy cancellation' is so clearly 'or ever' that 'o never' did not deserve to be suggested, even as a possible alternative?

On page 42 is the following: 'erased' in the manuscript 'and cancelled with pencil wave':

> *Heard in the hour of pausing voices,*
> *That brings the turning wheel to stand,*
> *When barges moor and windows glisten,*
> *And lights are faded in the land.*

Mr. Haber obligingly provides a facsimile of the page on which this quatrain was written. Judging from the facsimile alone, one would say that 'fasten' and not 'glisten' is the last word in line 3; certainly to print 'glisten' with not even a sign of interrogation is a dereliction of editorial duty. The superiority of 'fasten' has been pointed out in print elsewhere;[1] 'glisten', though not impossible, is inferior both in meaning and in sound. Even if Mr. Haber's ear and his intelligence did not tell him that 'fasten' was the better reading, his eye should have perceived that it ought at any rate to be recorded as an alternative.

On page 54 is the following characteristic couplet, found in the manuscript 'beneath wavy cancellation':

> *Better to think your friend's unkind*
> *Than know your lover's untrue.*

Is the 'cancellation' so ineffective that Mr. Haber can be certain that Housman wrote 'lover's' in line 2? And even if he wrote 'lover's', must not 'love's' have been what he intended? In either alternative, to print 'lover's' without a note or a question-mark argues a strange deafness to Housman's habitual rhythms.

---

[1] By me in the *Observer* 27 February 1955: 'Surely, feeling (for the whole stanza breathes a sense of things coming to rest), and reason (for windows do not glisten when lights are dim), and euphony (to echo "faded"), all cry out for "fasten"?' I may add that Mr. John Carter read the word as 'fasten', and so recorded it, when he examined the MS before it went to the United States.

Further evidence of such deafness on Mr. Haber's part is afforded by a fragment which he prints on page 91:

> *Stand back, you men and horses,*
> *You armies, turn and fly;*
> *You rivers, change your courses*
> *And climb the hills, or I*
> *Will know the reason why.*
>
> *Die above, O tempests brewing,*
> *I will have heaven serene;*
> *Despair, O tides, of doing*
> *The mischief that you mean,*
> *For I will stand between.*

The original is written, we are told, in 'faded ink, beneath wavy cancellation in heavy newer ink'. Did it never occur to Mr. Haber, on grounds of sound and sense, that 'above' should read 'down'? Is 'above' so clear, beneath the heavy ink cancellation, that it was right to print it without a question-mark? Mr. Haber should have heard the right reading even if he could not see it.

Perhaps the clearest proof of the laxity of Mr. Haber's editorial standards is afforded by the poem printed on page 94. Mr. Haber claims 'to reproduce as closely as type allows the display and position of the lines as they appear on the manuscript pages'. Comparison of page 94 with the facsimile of the corresponding manuscript page shows that, as regards this page, the claim is a false one: the printed page gives a misleading picture of the manuscript reproduced by the facsimile. How misleading, one asks, are the pages in Mr. Haber's book for which he gives us no facsimile to check them by? In this instance, Housman has made several attempts at the second stanza, in different places on the page; Mr. Haber, without giving any indication that he is doing so, gives us a conflated version of the text, incorporating from the alternative stanzas phrases which seem to have been rejected by the poet.

Worse than this, he reproduces falsely one of these tentative stanzas, omitting variants and actually mistranscribing a word. The facsimile reveals the following (we bracket and query readings which it leaves doubtful):

> (*November ?*)
> *October comes and carries*
> *More than*
> > *Life with the leaves*
> > *Eternal things away*
> > *Eternal things are (perished, ?)*
> > *The sense has left the letters*
> > *The tablet shall not stay*
> > *ir*

This is how Mr. Haber presents it:

> *October comes and carries*
> *Life with the leaves*
> *Eternal things away;*
> *Eternal things are perished,*
> *The sense has left the tablet.*
> *Their tablet shall not stay.*

Mr. Haber would presumably claim that his omission of two variants is justified by his own canon 'Alternative readings that were canceled are generally not given.' If that is accepted as an adequate defence in this particular case, we can only say that it reveals the indefensibility of the canon itself, for the variants he prints are just as much 'canceled' as those that he omits. And how is Mr. Haber to justify his punctuation, and his reading 'tablet' for 'letters' in the penultimate line?

What would Housman himself have said of such an editor? Very much, it may be imagined, what he said of one of those who preceded him in the editing of Lucan: '[He] was a born blunderer, marked cross from the womb and perverse; and he had not the shrewdness or modesty to suspect that others saw

clearer than he did.' An editor can hardly be accounted shrewd
if after years of study of the manuscripts he sees them less
clearly, at such points as those discussed above, than a reviewer who has spent a few hours on the text with no aid beyond
a couple of pages of facsimile; and even if the amendments
offered here are not certainly correct, an editor who does not
point out the possibility of an alternative to his own readings
in contexts such as these can hardly be accounted modest. Mr.
Haber certainly has not that saving grace; on only seven of the
sixty pages reproduced in his Part Two does he admit the
illegibility of a passage; in only five of the 500 or more lines
contained in that Part does he print the '?' that marks the
possible doubtfulness of his reading.

Let us turn from Mr. Haber's performance of his capital
task, the presentation of the text, to observe him as a commen-
tator on it:

> *Wake; the axe of morning shatters*
> *Shadows through. . . .*

> *Wake; the roof of shadows shatters*
> *Splintered on the plain it spanned*

The sense of these fragmentary alternatives, one would have
thought, is clear enough; but Mr. Haber must needs elucidate
it, with the brief note: 'Here *axe* means "axis".' Was a sillier
note, of equal length, ever penned?
Sometimes he supplements exposition with aesthetic comment:

> *How much more light than morning*
> *That soul alive bestows*
> *They know not that possess it*
> *But he that lost it knows.*

Mr. Haber devotes a footnote to telling us that 'the compacted
gall of this quatrain is the essence of A.E.H'.

Sometimes he essays a deeper note, as when he explains the inverted commas which (in the printed text but not in the manuscript) enclose the text of 'The Day of Battle': 'Why', asks Mr. Haber, 'were the signs of quotation added?' 'Because the text is put in the mouth of an imaginary soldier,' is the simple and sufficient answer. But it does not suffice Mr. Haber, who explains: 'Probably as a movement of retreat from the immediacy of the grim statement of the lyric (often left out even from the "soldiers' anthologies").' 'A similar motive', he adds, 'may have been behind the use of quotation marks about the heretical lyric number 47 of "The Carpenter's Son".' This last comment, with its naïve 'heretical', shows how far Mr. Haber is from beginning to understand the temper or the idiom of his author. Since it is hardly a part of his book to expound Housman's poetry or to appraise it, this insensitiveness does not have such serious results as do those defects of which we have already given evidence. But it can lead him astray. At one point he detects a 'phase of Orientalism' and at another, with equal fatuity, an 'Olympian air' in Housman's poetry; and the poem that he adjudges 'Olympian' he finds so reminiscent of his schoolboy verses that he is led to assign it to an early date, though it is in fact a quite ordinary example of Housman's mature rhetorical style.

Fortunately in his notes Mr. Haber confines himself for the most part to pointing out parallels and describing the actual condition of the manuscript. For such a task not much taste and not much intelligence is needed: it is enough to be able to write plain English. But plain English, unhappily, Mr. Haber is not content to write. This is how he tells us that Housman rubbed out or crossed out the variants that he rejected: 'The inept, faltering phrase thrown down in the haste of composition he savagely annihilated with the eraser or drowned in meandering ink'; and his description of the contents of the notebooks is enlivened by such observations as this: 'Those who put their trust in symbols may also find it worthy of remark that the last phrase we now read in his last notebook is "the grave".'

At times one wonders whether Mr. Haber's apparent inability to write plain English may be excused by an imperfect acquaintance with the written and even the spoken language. He comments, for instance, on Housman's preference for the spelling 'shew', saying that it makes the word 'a dubious rhyme with *overflow*', and concludes that it is 'probable' that Housman pronounced it 'show'. How else does he think that Housman could have pronounced it? He evidently thinks that to 'belabor' means to overwork, and that 'bequest' means gift; and what he thinks he means by 'obit' ('Laurence Housman's obit in the Analysis for the majority of these fragments is "Single lines and fragments"') and by 'omnipathy' ('an enthusiasm touched with a gleam of omnipathy') and by 'congelation' ('These few lines are further congelations of M.P. 33') we can but guess. As for Latin — a tongue with which an editor of Housman surely needs something more than a nodding acquaintance — for a specimen of Mr. Haber's competence in that language the reader may be referred to page 125.

Such solecisms as these demonstrate a lack of literacy which might be overlooked if Mr. Haber showed a deeper understanding or appreciation of his author; but even the possession of those attributes could not excuse the other editorial deficiencies to which attention has been called. We are forced to conclude that Mr. Haber exhibits what must be an almost unique combination of disqualifications for the task he has undertaken to perform. His preface contains the hint of a possible 'full-scale variorum edition' based on the 'rich material' still hidden in the Housman note-books. There are not a few first-rate English scholars in the United States well qualified to prepare such an edition with the delicacy that the task demands; if the Library of Congress intends to facilitate its appearance, and the Oxford University Press to sponsor its publication in

England (as it has sponsored Mr. Haber's volume), we hope that it is to one of these that the work will be entrusted.

The Housman Dilemma appeared in *The Times Literary Supplement* of 29 April 1955; on 1 August 1955 the *Literary Supplement* printed the following reply by Professor Haber and rejoinder from myself.

PROFESSOR HABER'S REPLY

Sir,— It must have been obvious to everyone who read the front-page article of *The Times Literary Supplement* for April 29 that it was not so much a review of my book, *The Manuscript Poems of A. E. Housman*, as a revelation of the peculiar animosities of the writer. Rather than essaying the tedious task of pointing out the many errors into which his ill temper has led him, I shall merely call attention to a few representative ones, feeling certain that your readers have already passed judgment on his many lapses from fact and good taste.

It is in the latter third of his article, where he attempts his most drastic criticism, that he makes his most patent blunders. Taking a dislike to the reading of some of Housman's lines as he finds them in my book, he proceeds to 'correct' them. What is his authority for this textual criticism? His intuition. Now this resort, though desperate, might be acceptable if he had nothing better to appeal to. But he wilfully turns his back upon the only authority that should be consulted in this case. All the manuscripts from which the challenged readings were taken are easily available and in a good state of preservation. Before publishing his objections he should have spent at least as much time in scrutinizing the manuscripts as he did in consulting his intuition. (Three minutes' 'thought' he hints sufficed for one clairvoyant exploit.)

He presumes to 'correct' another line by the naïve expedient of looking at the reproduction of a cancelled manuscript given on a nearby page. This attempt succeeds no better than the other but it is a move in the right direction. He should know — or should be able to guess if he does not know — that in reading photocopies of over-written manuscript, the original script is, in critical places, usually impossible to distinguish from the substituted lines or from whatever strokes or undulations that were used. Even clear pen copy cannot always be distinguished from pencil. It is difficult to imagine how anyone can expect to produce a respectable reading from the reproduction of a photograph and nearly impossible to imagine how any responsible person could have the effrontery to publish a reading obtained by such a method.

If my critic will abandon his methods and sit down with me over A. E. Housman's manuscripts in the Library of Congress, I shall humbly endeavour to show him that these lines and others he pretends to tamper with are printed as he finds them in my book, for the simple reason that A. E. Housman wrote them that way. In the meantime he might profitably read, or re-read, a lecture, 'The Application of Thought to Textual Criticism', published in the *Proceedings of the Classical Association*, August 1921, volume XVIII, pp. 67–84.

Passing from higher to lower concerns, the writer stops to suggest that there is only one accepted pronunciation for the word *shew* and quarrels with my comment that 'Housman probably pronounced the word "show".' If the complainant had taken the trouble to consult standard reference works, he would have found that, although some authorities allow only the pronunciation 'show', others admit 'shu'; and the *New Century Dictionary* prefers it. I mention this trifling error only as one illustration of how, in his eagerness to find fault, the writer here, as often elsewhere, makes a spectacle of himself by stumbling where the road is perfectly smooth except for the mole-hills of his own making.

From this point the writer at last falls to the level of personal abuse, to which he made frequent descents throughout the early stages of his article. As this attack, 'so strange, outrageous, and so variable', regularly misses its object or recoils

against its author, I shall make no reply to it except to call it
what it is; and there I shall leave him.

Columbus, Ohio, U.S.A. TOM BURNS HABER

The following was my Rejoinder:

In my review I recorded my opinion that Mr. Haber, as an
editor, showed himself to be lacking in candour, overconfident,
not a dependable transcriber, incapable of fully appreciating
the tone and idiom of his author, and not literate in his writing
of English. I supported my strictures by a selection from the
many errors and solecisms in his book. Mr. Haber has chosen
not to answer my criticisms. Readers can draw their own conclusions.

One of the faults I imputed to Mr. Haber was a lack of 'the
intellectual humility that confesses the doubtfulness of a doubtful reading'. I pointed out that in only five of the 500 lines in
his Part II did he admit that doubt might be cast upon his text.
I gave five examples of places where it seemed to me that the
reading printed by Mr. Haber was, to say the least, doubtful,
and suggested an alternative which my 'intuition' told me that
Housman must, or might, have written. Since in each case the
text was overscored, sometimes heavily and in ink, the possibility of a mis-reading was surely to be reckoned with. I am
sorry that space does not permit me to quote the passages in
question. I will, however, give an additional example in order to
make plain the main issue between Mr. Haber and myself.
On page 34 of his text, Mr. Haber prints the following stanza,
over-scored in the manuscript by 'wavy cancellation in ink':

With odours from the graves of balm
That far away it fanned,
And whispering of the plumy palm
It moved in morning land.

My 'intuition' tells me that Housman must, or might well, have
written 'groves' in line 1; and I ask, 'Did it not occur to Mr.

Haber that *groves* might be the right reading? Is *graves* so clearly written in the manuscript that Mr. Haber was right to print it without even the question-mark that indicates the possibility of doubt?' Repeatedly in my review I asked exactly similar questions. A true scholar would surely have referred to the manuscript and given a straight answer to each such challenge. Mr. Haber contents himself with railing (not, I must say, very politely) at the 'effrontery' of a critic who dares to question an editor's readings in reliance on his own critical judgment.

Mr. Haber says that it is unsafe to rely on facsimiles. So it is; but sometimes it is quite plain even from a facsimile that an editor has departed widely from the text before him. One of the two facsimiles given by Mr. Haber shows quite plainly that he has not printed the text so as to reproduce (as he claims to do) 'as clearly as type allows the display and position of the lines as they appear on the manuscript pages'. It is no answer to this criticism to say that facsimiles do not enable one to detect *minutiae*.

I should add a word about 'shew', the one point on which Mr. Haber attempts to answer a specific criticism made by me.

Housman often used the old-fashioned spelling 'shew'; Mr. Haber says that this 'would have made a dubious rhyme to *overflow*'; although (he adds) Housman 'probably pronounced the word "show".' It seemed to me silly to suggest that because Housman sometimes spelt the word 'shew' he might sometimes (or always) have pronounced it 'shu'; in my opinion, he could only have pronounced it 'show', to rhyme with 'overflow', how-ever he spelt it. The fact that an American dictionary recognizes an alternative pronunciation (which the Oxford Dictionary does not) does not lead me to change this opinion.

*

POSTSCRIPT

Mr. Haber, in consenting to the publication of his reply, stipulated for the omission of his last two sentences, which were perhaps somewhat intemperate in tone. I would have been glad to mitigate the severity of some of my own comments, for I feel no personal animosity against Mr. Haber; but I think it better to leave my article, for the record, exactly as I wrote it; I have slightly abbreviated my rejoinder.

I now suggest two further corrections, in two stanzas printed on page 94 of *The Manuscript Poems of A. E. Housman:*

> *So here I bring the auger*
> *And in the hole I drill*
> *I pour out all the evil,*
> *The vitriol sure to kill.*

> *Next year in our green woodland*
> *Shall stand a naked tree,*
> *Where spring comes north and islands*
> *Turn leafy in the sea.*

I have been shown a copy made by Laurence Housman of a version of this poem in which the third line of the first stanza quoted above reads 'I pour out of the vial', and 'Where spring' in the third line of the next stanza reads 'When spring'. Scrutiny of the facsimile facing page 83 of Mr. Haber's book confirms the first of these readings (one can identify the 'f' in 'of', and the dot over the 'i' fits 'vial' and not 'evil') and does not contradict the second. Here again Mr. Haber might surely have at least indicated the doubtfulness of the text he printed.

A Polish Plagiarist

*

I

In 1958 I published an article in *Oxford Slavonic Papers*[1] concerning the *Silviludia* of the seventeenth-century Polish Jesuit poet Casimir Sarbiewski. Sarbiewski is one of the glories of the Renaissance literature of Poland, and since my article was an attempt to prove that the *Silviludia*, a series of poems that had won him much praise for its (supposed) originality, was in fact stolen *en bloc* and without acknowledgment from a contemporary Italian, I anticipated that its publication might, at any rate in the small circle of those interested in the Latin poetry of the Renaissance, create something of a stir. In the event, my attempted demonstration was accepted as successful,[2] and its impact upon Polish critical opinion was likened by more than one reviewer to that of an atomic bomb.[3]

[1] viii. 1–48.

[2] 'Depuis longtemps on ressentait un certain malaise devant les *Silviludia* de Mathieu-Casimir Sarbiewski . . . John Sparrow a donné le mot de l'énigme en établissant de manière irréfutable qu'ils constituent un plagiat presque continu . . .', Backvis, *Revue des études slaves*, xxxvi (1959), 287; 'The reason why the poet refrained from publishing this work has only recently been discovered: the whole cycle of 10 poems — as John Sparrow has demonstrated — was taken without alteration from the pastoral drama *Ludovicus* . . . In the face of this discovery, any attempt to present Sarbiewski as the creator of a new literary genre and a new metre is doomed to failure', Fr. Paul Rabikauskas, S. J., in *Lietuviu enciklopedija* xxvi, 492–3 (tr.); 'Why then did not Sarbiewski publish the work himself? . . . J. Sparrow alone has given a convincing answer to this question: Sarbiewski could not publish the poem, for most of it (including its title) was taken from the Baroque drama *Ludovicus*', Stefan Zabłocki, *Eos*, l (1959/60), fasc. 2 (tr.); see also Wiktor Weintraub in *Wiadomości* (London), 825 (1962), 4, and Robert A. Maguire in *The Polish review* iv (1959), 143–4. Julian Krzyżanowski's article in *Ruch literacki* is referred to below.

[3] See Śmieja in *Wiadomości* (London), (1958), 5 and St. Seliga in *Tydzień Polski* (London), 52/55 (1959), 14.

89

The tone of the reviews in which the discovery was received in Poland, however, reassured me that the explosion of this particular bomb, although it had done some damage to the reputation of a national literary figure, had not exacerbated hostilities between East and West, and the *doyen* of Polish literary history and criticism, Professor Julian Krzyżanowski, in his article '*A pia fraus* of Sarbiewski',[1] was particularly generous in his judgment of my work. Professor Krzyżanowski recalled his own 'youthful and enthusiastic encounter' with the *Silviludia* amid the snows of a Siberian winter more than forty years before, and described how an article of his inspired by that encounter helped to establish the poems as 'one of the leading works of Polish Baroque poetry', and how in 1934 R. Ganszyniec published an edition of them with a thorough introductory study, and in 1939 the famous classical scholar Tadeusz Sinko wrote an article discussing their possible connexion with Italian drama. All this work, said Professor Krzyżanowski, was to be brought to nothing by the 'sensational discovery' announced in my article, the conclusions of which must be accepted. But he made one reservation. While agreeing that the *Silviludia* that we know must have been taken from Mario Bettini's pastoral drama *Ludovicus*, he questioned whether one could say for certain that it was these *Silviludia* that Sarbiewski had claimed as his own composition. Sarbiewski had written to his friend Stanisław Łubieński, Bishop of Płock, about a 'liber Sylviludiorum' which he said he had just composed in an access of inspiration, and I had assumed that this referred to the *Silviludia* we know (nothing else of Sarbiewski's having come down to us under this title or suitable to be called by it) and that Sarbiewski must therefore be convicted not only of copying these poems from another writer, but also of trying to pass them off as his own.

Professor Krzyżanowski suggested that my assumption might have been too hasty. 'A conjecture may be put forward', he wrote (I quote in translation), 'that the "liber Sylviludiorum"

[1] *Ruch literacki*, 1960, no. 1–2.

A Polish Plagiarist

about which Sarbiewski wrote to Łubieński is perhaps something other than the *Silviludia* copied from Bettini's drama; a similar, but different, work. In the result, then,' he concluded, 'while I subscribe to J. Sparrow's arguments about the *Silviludia* known in print, one may retain some doubt whether Sarbiewski should be accused of plagiarism; some other 'Silviludia', which we do not know today, may be relevant here. His future biographer will have to think about this matter'.

This suggestion of Professor Krzyżanowski's was taken up in a long and powerful article published in the Italian journal *Ricerche slavistiche*[1] by Fr. Józef Warszawski, S. J., who sought to show that what Professor Krzyżanowski put forward as a conjecture is capable of irrefutable demonstration.

According to Fr. Warszawski,[2] there must have been two series of poems: (1) a skilful adaptation from Bettini, composed by S. in 1636[3] and never (so far as is known) claimed by him as his own original work — these are the *Silviludia* that have come down to us; (2) a series of original poems which have not survived, composed by S. in 1637 and referred to by him in his letters of that year to Łubieński as a 'liber Sylviludiorum'.

There is, therefore, according to W., nothing false or insincere in the claims made by S. in his letters about the vanished 'liber Sylviludiorum', for these were indeed entirely his own work; and, as for the poems that have survived, he had no reason to be ashamed of them either, for they were a skilful piece of literary adaptation; he never pretended (says W.) that they were anything else; and it was as such, he suggests, that they were admired and enjoyed by King Władysław and his Court, for whom they were written.

W.'s article is closely reasoned, and even if it did not contain a most generous tribute to my work, I should wish to praise its author for the skill with which he presents his own arguments,

[1] x (Rome, 1962), 22–74.
[2] For brevity's sake I shall henceforward in this article refer to Fr. Warszawski as 'W.' and to Sarbiewski as 'S.'.
[3] And, in the case of *Silviludium* IX, the 'Silviludium prenuziale', in 1637 (see below).

and thank him for the courtesy with which he criticizes mine. His arguments, indeed, may carry conviction up to the point already reached by Professor Krzyżanowski when he said that S. *might* in his letters have been referring to another set of *Silviludia*; but when W. goes further and seeks to show that this *must* have been so, then I have in honesty to say that I think he goes too far; indeed, most careful consideration of his article leaves me only the more convinced of the correctness of the position that I assumed (perhaps too hastily) in my own.

II

To do justice to W.'s criticisms, I must briefly recapitulate the relevant facts.

S. was born in 1595; he entered the Society of Jesus in 1612; ten years later he spent some three years (1622–5) in Rome. Returning to Poland, he taught rhetoric, philosophy, and theology in the University of Vilna, until in 1635 he was summoned to be chaplain and preacher to the Court of Władysław IV at Warsaw, where he died in 1640.

Already during his lifetime S. was celebrated all over Europe for his Latin lyrics, of which nearly fifty editions were published before 1700. His popularity continued well into the succeeding century, and his influence impressed itself in particular upon a number of English poets; in the nineteenth century he was greatly admired by Landor and by Coleridge.

Most of S.'s poetry consisted of Odes on the Horatian model, and it was on these that his fame — he was known as 'Horatius Sarmaticus' — chiefly depended. The *Silviludia*, a series of ten lyrical pieces, of an average length of some forty lines, are entirely different in character from the rest of his work; they are (as Thomas Warton said of Cowley's Latin verse) 'worthy of the pastoral pencil of Watteau' — songs and choruses meant to be sung while shepherds, huntsmen, and fishermen danced ballets, evidently for the delectation of the Court of King Władysław, whose approaching marriage is the theme of one of them. There is nothing classical about these poems; their metres are mainly (if not entirely) accentual, their language and imagery are Marinistic and Baroque. Not only are they utterly unlike anything else in S.'s work, but (according to historians of Polish literature) they are utterly unlike anything that had till then come from the pen of any Polish writer.

The explanation of this new departure in S.'s style and metre is, as I showed in my article, that he took his text, with practically no substantial alteration and with the addition of only a score or so of lines, from a pastoral drama, Mario Bettini's *Ludovicus*, which had attained great popularity in Italy in the decade preceding S.'s visit to Rome, and which had been published for the first time in the year (1622) of his arrival there. No doubt he took a copy of this edition back with him to Poland. The fact that the text was not his own work no doubt explains why the *Silviludia* were not included in any edition of S.'s poems published during his lifetime.

Not only were the *Silviludia* unpublished during S.'s lifetime; they remained in manuscript for more than a century after his death; then, almost simultaneously and quite independently, there appeared two editions of S.'s works — one (edited by Adam Naruszewicz, S. J.) in Vilna in 1757, the other (in the elegant series of Latin poets published by Barbou) in Paris in 1759 — each of which contained a text of the *Silviludia*, printed from a different manuscript source. The differences between the Paris and the Vilna texts are not numerous, nor (subject to what is said below) are they important.

The only known mention by S. of any 'Silviludia' are the passages in his letters to Łubieński already referred to: on 4 November 1637 he declares that while attending the King on a recent hunting expedition in the district of Strzembowo he withdrew to a primitive cabin ('vili humilique tuguriolo') at Płońsk near by, where he was visited by a strain of inspiration under the influence of which he wrote a collection of sylvan recreations ('librum Sylviludiorum'); these poems, he says, were at the time of writing his letter in the hands of the King; he adds that they were novel both in style and in metre ('novo et metro et stylo'). On 17 December S. writes that the poems were now with 'Symphoniaci Musicique nostri', who were (presumably) setting them to music; a fortnight later he declares that he owes the *Silviludia* and the mood that inspired them to Łubieński's hospitality in his town and country houses at 'Viscovium' and 'Brocovium', and also to his own rural seclusion in his cabin at Płońsk and the fresh and genial climate of his native village of Sarbievo. Both Płońsk and Sarbievo are in fact, as W. points out, in the neighbourhood of Strzembowo.

Finally, on 7 January 1638, S. sends his friend his only manuscript of the poems, likening them to embroideries of hunting-scenes in Flemish tapestries; just as the woven pictures are uniformly green, so (he says) his *Silviludia* are almost all vernal ('pene omnia verna sunt'). In reply, Łubieński declares that the poems have given him intense pleasure; he has copied them out (he says) and sends his copy to the poet.

'One thing', I wrote in my original article, 'emerges plainly from this correspondence: S. is claiming that he wrote the *Silviludia* himself, inspired by the surroundings of his native village; the only other debts that he acknowledges with reference to their composition are his debts to the hospitality of Łubieński in the town and in the country and to his own "lyricus impetus".' In writing thus, I assumed that the *Silviludia* referred to were the *Silviludia* that have come down to us, which had in fact been taken from Bettini. What are W.'s grounds for challenging this assumption?

III

The main basis of W.'s case is a fact to which in my article I attached no particular significance: to most of the *Silviludia* S. prefixed titles relating to places where the action is supposed to occur: e.g. *Silv.* I: *Cum . . . Rex Berstos venatum veniret; Silv.* II: *Saltus Pastorum, cum Vladislaus Solecznicos mane venatum prodiret; Silv.* III: *Dum Vladislaus Kotrae venatur; Silv.* IV: *Ad Auram ut labores et aestum temperet Vladislao in campis Merecensibus sub meridiem venanti*; and so on.

A Polish Plagiarist

W. shows, illustrating his demonstration from a contemporary map, that all the places so referred to — Berszty, Soleczniki, Kotra, Lejpuny, Lake Metel — are in the district of Merecz, which lies between Vilna and Grodno. He goes on to point out that surviving records prove that the King did not go on a hunting expedition in the Merecz district in 1637, the year to which S.'s letters to Łubieński refer the composition of his 'liber *Sylviludiorum*'. 'Tutte le fonti storiche', he writes, 'concordano nel fatto che, nel periodo 1635–40, cioè nel periodo in cui il Sarbiewski era a fianco del re in qualità di suo predicatore di corte, il re Władysław solo due volte effettuò partite di caccia nella regione di Merecz: la prima volta nel 1636, la seconda nel 1639.'

Upon this basis, W.'s argument proceeds as follows. The *Silviludia* (or at any rate the seven of them that contain in their titles the name of a place) must have been performed each of them at the place and time and on the occasion indicated in its title — *Silviludium* II, for instance, *Saltus Pastorum, cum Vladislaus Solecznicos mane venatum prodiret*, was a dance of shepherds that must have been actually performed early in the morning when the King was setting off to hunt at Soleczniki; *Silviludium* X, *Cantus Zephyri, Vladislao sub vesperum Leypunos venienti*, must have been sung at Lejpuny when the King arrived there in the evening; and so on. In each case, says W., the particulars in the title are so precise that they cannot be a mere literary fiction, but must refer to an actual performance given at the time and place, and on the occasion, specified.

Since the occasions for these performances can only have occurred in 1636, because this (apart from 1639)[1] was the one

[1] W. consistently assumes that 1636 must have been the date of the composition of the '*Silviludia* of Merecz', though the King was hunting in the Merecz district also in 1639, according to the evidence cited by him. I suppose that W. rules out the latter year because it would not fit in with his theory; we should then have to suppose that S. (1) adapted *Silv.* IX (the '*Silviludium* prenuziale') from Bettini in Aug. 1637; (2) composed the '*Silviludia* of Strzembowo' 'novo et metro et stylo' in Oct. 1637; (3) resumed his adaptations from Bettini with *Silv.* I–VIII and X of the '*Silviludia* of Merecz' in 1639 — a sequence of events entirely lacking in plausibility.

year during the relevant period when the King is known to have hunted in the neighbourhood of Merecz, W. argues that it must have been in that year that the pieces were composed (or, rather, adapted), and therefore S.'s letters of 1637 claiming originality for the 'liber Sylviludiorum' that he had then just completed, must refer to some other compositions; they accordingly afford no proof that he concealed the true source of the *Silviludia* that have come down to us.

It is evident that this argument depends for its force upon the assumption that S.'s title for each *Silviludium* refers to the circumstances of its performance and not only to its subject matter. To hold the latter, W. repeatedly asserts — e.g. to treat *Silv.* II as a dance *representing* shepherds dancing before the King when he was setting off to hunt at Soleczniki — would be to reduce the *Silviludia* to mere literary fictions; the references in the titles, he says, are far too precise to allow that to be the case — 'Il titolo *Vladislao sub vesperum Leypunos venienti* indica una concreta, inequivocabile persona storica, un concreto luogo geografico e concreto, inequivocabile caso storico. Non puo indicare una finzione letteraria, dato che e affatto concreto. Il *Silviludium* che porta tale titolo deve essere riconosciuto come realmente "*actually performed*" e ciò nel giorno in cui "il re Władysław IV giunse verso sera a Leypuny". La stessa cosa vale per gli altri *Silviludia*'.

My answer to this contention is twofold. First, it does not seem to me to be at all unlikely that S. should have composed (or adapted) at Strzembowo in 1637 a series of songs and dances re-enacting or recalling events that had actually taken place during a hunting expedition in another district a year or more before. A masque written for performance at Court in Warsaw in 1637 might well be designed to bring before the eyes of the courtiers a series of events, typical or actual, belonging to a hunting expedition that had taken place during the preceding year at Merecz. Why not? A masque at Hampton Court or Whitehall might well re-enact incidents from a Royal progress in an earlier year through the towns of (say) Leicestershire or

Lincolnshire, or events of the monarch's last hunting foray in the forests of Windsor or Nottingham.

The first part of my answer to W. on this point, therefore, is that, giving full significance to the titles of the individual pieces, I see nothing improbable in the hypothesis that the *Silviludia* were a literary 'fiction' in the sense and to the extent indicated in the preceding paragraph.

The second part of my answer is that I see great difficulties in the alternative hypothesis, viz. that the songs and dances comprised in the *Silviludia* were composed for and performed on the actual occasions indicated in their titles. Even assuming that the programme of the chase was so exactly laid down that S. could anticipate and prepare a set of verses for the King's departure for Soleczniki in the early morning or his arrival at Lejpuny in the evening, are we really to suppose that all the requisite dramatic apparatus was at hand upon the plains of Merecz or the banks of the River Kotra or of Lake Metel? And even if the apparatus had been available — the musicians, the singers, the dancers, the actors, the costumes, the musical instruments, the stage properties — can it really have been the King's pleasure, when he was brushing with hasty steps the dews away on a dawn hunting expedition, or returning in the evening with the sweat of the chase upon his brow, to be stopped in his tracks, with all his retinue of the chase, in order that they should be spectators of the performance of an elaborate Latin pantomime?[1]

Is it not more likely that S. offered the King, after the whole expedition had come to an end, a *divertissement* that strung together a series of episodes relating to places actually visited

---

[1] In my original article I described the *Silviludia* as 'intended for the entertainment of Władisław IV of Poland during hunting expeditions'. I confess that I did not give much thought to the circumstances of their performance, which seemed irrelevant to my main topic; had I done so, I should not have written this sentence, but would have contented myself with saying (as I did) that they were prepared as a '*divertissement* for the Polish court' and that no record survives 'to show whether the poems were actually set to music and performed, as it was evidently intended that they should be'.

during the course of it, the whole being performed on a proper stage, presumably at the Court in Warsaw?

The *Silviludia* as we have them fit better with this hypothesis, for they contain two pieces (V and VI) that carry no indications of their being related to any particular place (W. does not make it clear how these fit into his scheme); and, as W. himself points out, the opening and closing pieces of the series, in the order that he accepts as authentic,[1] contain internal marks of being the first and last of a series — marks that would lose their significance if the poems were performed each of them at a different time and place from any other.

One *Silviludium* (IX in the Paris, X in the Vilna, edition) demands separate consideration. It is entitled *Cantus et Saltus Messorum, venante paulo ante regias nuptias Vladislao.*

Władysław's marriage to Cecilia Renata, daughter of the Emperor Ferdinand II, took place in Warsaw on 12 September 1637. W. quotes a contemporary letter proving that the King was away on a hunting expedition, half a day's journey from Warsaw, on 8 August 1637, and this is no doubt the expedition referred to in the title to *Silv.* IX; where it took place is uncertain, but it cannot have been in the district of Merecz, for that (according to W.) is some 300 kilometres distant from Warsaw. W., therefore, true to his principle that the poem must have been written at the time and performed at the place specified in or indicated by its title, has to admit that this *Silviludium* is separated both by date and by place from the series that he calls 'the *Silviludia* of Merecz',[2] and his hypothesis involves the following time-table:

---

[1] *Silviludia* X and VIII in the Paris edition, I and IX in the edition of Vilna (which W. argues, with some plausibility, preserves the original order); *Silviludium* X in the Vilna edition, according to W., is *extra ordinem* and does not belong to the series (see below).

[2] A conclusion that he finds to be confirmed by its position at the end of the series as preserved in the Vilna edition.

A Polish Plagiarist

Title	Date of Compo- sition	Place of Composition or Performance	Source
(1) *Silviludia* I–VIII, X[1]	Sept. 1636	Merecz	Bettini's '*Tragicum Sylviludium*'
(2) *Silviludium* IX ('prenuziale')[2]	Aug. 1637	? (not Merecz)	Bettini's '*Tragicum Sylviludium*'
(3) 'liber Sylviludi- orum'	Oct. 1637	Strzembowo	Original: 'novo et stylo et metro'.

My own hypothesis is simpler: the 'liber Sylviludiorum' that S. composed in or about October 1637 was a unity, weaving into a single series a number of songs, all of them adapted from Bettini, that recalled not only the King's 'pre-nuptial' hunting expedition of a month or so before but also episodes belonging to his last hunting expedition in Merecz during the previous year.

W.'s time-table is open to two objections, one less serious, the other practically fatal.

First, on W.'s hypothesis we must suppose that S. manu- factured a series of adaptations of Bettini, which he called *Silviludia*, in September 1636; that he again had recourse to Bettini when producing something for the King's impending marriage in August 1637; and that, a month or so after that, he composed another series of 'hunting' poems, unrelated to Bettini, to which he gave the same title. That is not impossible, but it hardly seems a likely sequence of events.

But W.'s hypothesis involves a much greater difficulty than that. S. described his 'liber Sylviludiorum' of 1637 as 'novo et metro et stylo'. This description obviously fits exactly the *Silviludia* that we know. But what can it have meant in its

---

[1] *Silv.* I–IX in the Vilna edition.   [2] *Silv.* X in the Vilna edition.

application to W.'s 'Silviludia of Strzembowo' if his time-table
is accepted? Accentual verses on the Bettini model would, on
W.'s hypothesis, no longer be a novelty in 1637, classical verses
from S.'s pen, of course, still less so; therefore we have to
suppose that S., having in August 1637 completed a *Silviludium*
(the 'prenuziale') on the Bettini model, a month or so later
produced a further series of *Silviludia* that were neither classical nor Bettinian, but something that could still be called 'new,
both in style and metre'. These were praised by Łubieński and
approved by the King to be set to music by the Court
musicians — and then they vanish into thin air. What can
these fresh novelties — neither classical nor Baroque — have
been like? In what kind of metre — neither quantitative nor
accentual — can they have been written? And how is it that
we hear no more about them? Is it not particularly strange that
S.'s adaptations should have survived and his original *Silviludia*, which must have been remarkable novelties, should
have silently disappeared?

IV

W.'s remaining arguments are mainly directed to showing (1)
that the surviving *Silviludia* bear the marks of being not
plagiarisms but self-confessed adaptations; (2) that they do not
answer the description of the 'liber Sylviludiorum' given by S.
in his letters.

(1) W. insists that the *Silviludia* are a particularly skilful
work of adaptation, of which S. had reason to feel proud rather
than ashamed. For my part, I should say rather that they are a
piece of somewhat jejune plagiarism: the alterations made by
S. are very few in number, most of them are trifling or merely
mechanical (e.g. *Ludovicus* becomes *Vladislaus* — fortunately
its metrical equivalent), and almost as often as not they do
violence to the metre of the original, which S. evidently did not
understand.

By a bold paradox W. claims that the fact that the changes
are few is itself a sign that S. offered the work openly as an

adaptation of a known original; the literary thief, he says, disguises his loot as thoroughly as he can (as gipsies, according to Macaulay, mutilate the children they steal so as to be able to pass them off as their own); the adapter, on the other hand, is proud if he can fit his original to its new use with little or no alteration. Therefore, says W., the fact that S. made only minimal changes in Bettini's text is an indication that he was openly adapting it, and not trying to pass it off as his own original work.

There is another, surely more plausible, explanation. If the plagiarist alters his original, it is for fear of discovery; where he is confident that his readers are not acquainted with it, the need for alteration — at any rate, extensive alteration — disappears. Now there was in fact small risk that anyone in Poland — including even the learned Łubieński — would know Bettini's work or even know of its existence; although his two *favole boschereccie* (*Rubenus* and *Ludovicus*) were popular in Italy and had several times been performed upon the Italian stage, printed editions of them were evidently (as they still are) very rare; *Rubenus* was already in the 1630's almost unprocurable even in Northern Italy: 'Vivunt adhuc', writes Giacomo Mazzini in 1632, 'viri nobilitate, ac doctrina insignes, qui ut exemplum unum Hilarotragoediae (*Rubenus*) a Bibliopola exprimerent Cremonae, alter vicenas libras, alter circiter quinquagenas monetae eius regionis impenderint: tantum argenti pro eo opusculo.' There was, then, small chance that the King or the Court would ever have seen a copy of *Ludovicus;* as for his literary friend Łubieński, S. no doubt knew well enough whether he was acquainted with Bettini's work, and would not have risked the deception if he had been.

W.'s picture of an audience sufficiently familiar with the original to appreciate the skill with which S. had performed his task of adaptation is at variance with all probability. And even if the courtiers had been familiar with Bettini's play, what opportunity would they have had, since S.'s text was not available in print, of making the detailed comparison necessary if they were to appreciate S.'s 'skill' as an adapter? Granted that, *per impossibile*, these conditions were fulfilled, the alterations made by S. were in fact, as I have pointed out, not such as were likely to have evoked their admiration or anybody else's; indeed, I find it hard to suppose that S. would ever have dared openly to offer such crude reproductions of another's work for the entertainment of the Court, particularly in celebration of so important an event as the King's approaching marriage.

(2) W.'s second line of argument is based on the contention that the *Silviludia* that have come down to us do not correspond to the description appearing in the letters to Łubieński. In the first place, he says, they were not a work of inspiration; least of all could they have been inspired in the confines of a hut in wintry surroundings at Strzembowo, when they are all about summer happenings near Merecz, and the poet represents himself as wandering freely 'per prata ac sylvas'. Therefore, says W., S. could not in fact have been referring to the *Silviludia* we know; furthermore, if he had indeed described the '*Silviludia* of Merecz' in his letters as inspired productions, Łubieński, the King, and the Court could not have failed to notice the discrepancy, and to overwhelm the poet with ridicule on account of them.[1]

The first part of this argument is a plain *petitio principii*: it may be, as W. says, that no two things more completely exclude each other than inspiration and plagiarism:[2] and if so,

---

[1] In particular, says W. (p. 61), the idea of composing a poem representing the King hunting 'paulo ante regias nuptias' at a date after the marriage had taken place, and the attempt to get it set to music after the conclusion of the nuptial celebrations, 'avrebbero certamente provocato le beffe di tutta la corte'.

[2] 'Bisogna dichiarare che nulla si esclude a vicenda come l'ispirazione e il plagio, l'opera nata dall'ispirazione e quella copiata. Se i *Silviludia* di Merecz — come ha dimostrato il prof. Sparrow — sono quasi interamente ripresi dal Bettini, essi non costituiscono un'opera nata dall'ispirazione. Quindi tale opera, postulata dalla dichiarazione del Sarbiewski, si deve considerare come un circlo completamente diverso da quello dei *Silviludia di* Merecz'

S. certainly could not have truly declared that his thefts from Bettini were inspired. But it is not (unfortunately) necessary to suppose that S. was telling the truth when he claimed in his letters that the *Silviludia* were a work of inspiration; the suggestion is that he was pretending he was inspired when in fact he was not. No such contradiction as W. alleges arises if we suppose that S. was disingenuously concealing his theft.

I turn therefore to the second branch of W.'s argument: viz., that the deception must have been evident to Łubieński, the King, and the Court, even if they were unacquainted with Bettini's work; they could not (says W.) have failed to observe the discrepancy between the plainly uninspired '*Silviludia* of Merecz' and the claims made about the inspired origin of the poems referred to in S.'s letters.

So far as the King and the Court are concerned, this assumes that they were aware of the contents of S.'s letters to the Bishop — surely a most improbable assumption.[1] But even if the King and his entourage were aware of the relevant passages in S.'s letters, I see no reason why they, or Łubieński, should have felt that any discrepancy or anomaly was involved. They would surely not have taken S.'s claim to be 'inspired' as seriously, or as literally, as W. suggests. Poets who speak of being inspired by their surroundings, or by a divine 'afflatus', do not expect to be taken *au pied de la lettre* — and it is to be noted, in this case, that S. did not say that he was inspired to describe his actual surroundings; he merely described the circumstances in which inspiration came upon him, and he acknowledged also his indebtedness, in composing the *Sil-viludia*, to the comforts of Łubieński's town and country

---

[1] W. quotes from Th. Wall (*M. C. Sarbiewski ... Poemata Omnia* (Starawiescz, 1892), pp. xv–xvi) one or two passages from the correspondence between S. and Łubieński in which each writer deplores the fact that their letters are opened by unknown persons and made available to others. But this is a long way from justifying the assumption that everything in S.'s letters (including his description of the circumstances in which he composed the *Silviludia*) must have been generally known at Court.

houses. As for the 'afflatus', the inspiration of poetry — even poetry far more deeply felt than the *Silviludia* can claim to be — may be emotion recollected in subsequent tranquillity, and S. might well have been inspired, both when staying with Łubieński and in his cabin at Strzembowo to imagine in autumn the forests and lakes of Merecz, and his perambulations of them, in a previous spring or summer.

I can see no inconsistency, therefore, and no reason for supposing that S.'s contemporaries would have detected any, between the *Silviludia* that we know, with all their summer scenes, and S.'s claim that he was inspired to write them in autumnal surroundings.[1]

The lack of inspiration, however, is not the only feature of the *Silviludia* that would, according to W., have troubled Łubieński, or anyone reading them in the light of S.'s description of them in his letters. They would also have detected an irreconcilable discrepancy between the poems and the passage in which S. says that they treated of hunting against a spring background. S.'s words are these:

'Sed ut peristromata illa Belgica, quae venationes exhibent, uno prope modum colore atque eo quidem viridi contexuntur; ita haec Sylviludia pene omnia verna sunt.'

This description, says W., obviously does not fit the *Silviludia* that we know, because they contain no actual description of hunting-scenes, and the background against which they are set is one of trees in full summer leaf.

No doubt the reference to the hunting-scenes in Belgian tapestries would be irrelevant if the poems to which S. likened them were not concerned with hunting; but he does not say explicitly, nor (I think) does he imply, that his poems actually described the incidents of the chase; what he does say is surely satisfied by the three or four references to hunting in the text,

---

[1] I cannot help observing that, if W. is right, the same suspicion would have been aroused by the 'Silviludia of Strzembowo' if S. rightly described them as 'pene omnia verna': they were 'inspired' poems composed in October, and yet they treated of the spring.

quoted by W.,[1] and by the fact that eight of the ten poems contain references to hunting in their titles.

As for the phrase 'pene omnia verna sunt', I suspect that S. was not a very faithful painter of nature; spring and summer flowers are confounded in the floral profusion of his landscapes, and, though there is a feeling throughout of mid-summer heat ('Rutilo latrat Sirius astro' *Silv.* IV, 4–5), the dominant colour, as S. declares, is green, and it is in the spring-time that the King's arrival at Lejpuny is supposed to take place in *Silv.* X (30–33):

> *Hic Tellus per me verno*
> *Crinita flore comitur,*
> *Hic virides blanditur*
> *Fucata genas, colorata vultus.*

Here again, I suggest that W. has attached to expressions contained in S.'s letters a precise meaning that they were not intended to bear, and that would never have been attached to them by his contemporaries.

v

W. advances in support of his hypothesis two subsidiary arguments which can be briefly dealt with.

The poems referred to in the letters to Łubieński, he points out, are described as 'liber Sylviludiorum'; the surviving poems have come down to us in three texts, a manuscript[2] in which the series is entitled simply *Silviludia*; the Paris edition of 1759, in which it is entitled *Silviludia poetica*; and the Vilna edition of 1757, in which it is entitled *Silviludia dithyrambica*. The manuscripts from which the printed texts are derived, says W., must

---

[1] 'Venatores ducite' *Silv.* II, 38–9; 'Nec venatus Regii Cedit labor' *Silv.* IV, 7–8; 'Annue nostro ... venatu' *Silv.* VI, 40, 49; 'Venatuum potenti Se prata Ladislao Leypunensia comant' *Silv.* X, 13–15; 'Tu grande Vladislai, Vicina dum venatico Exercet arva cursu, Nomen ... persones' *Silv.* VIII, 61–5.

[2] See Jan Oko, *Rękopis wileński 'Zabaw leśnych'* Sarbiewskiego (Vilna, 1929).

either have contained the published titles, or no title at all; which ever of these hypotheses is accepted, 'non combia il fatto che il titolo *liber Sylviludiorum*, ricordato da Sarbiewski, non si trova in nessuno dei manoscritti' (W., p. 55). I find it hard to take this seriously as an argument that the work preserved in the manuscripts is not the same as that referred to in the letter; it is enough, surely, to point out that S. in his letter was not professing to confer a title upon the work, he was simply describing it; and I can see no reason why the text of the collection of poems described by its author as 'liber Sylviludiorum' should not have been preserved in manuscript under the title 'Silviludia', with or without the addition of such epithets as 'poetica' or 'dithyrambica'.

Finally, W. adduces an *a priori* argument founded on what he calls 'l'elemento psicologico'. S. was the author of two treatises on poetical composition, the fruits of his professorship of rhetoric: *De perfecta poesi*[1] and *Praecepta poetica*.[2] W. (p. 49) calls attention to a passage in *De perfecta poesi* in which S. declares that he has used an analysis that he has found in Scaliger, but has altered it somewhat and improved upon it 'ne quidquam de alieno sumpsisse videamur'; in the *Praecepta poetica* he says that he has abstained from treating a certain topic 'ne ... molestissimam cramben repetere videamur *et aliquid ex alieno mutuari — a quo semper maxime afuimus*'. If we take these declarations (says W.) in conjunction with the fact that S. is always sincere and open in his letters to Łubieński, and the fact that throughout his critical disquisitions he betrays extreme personal diffidence (in support of which W. quotes a number of phrases expressive of S.'s modesty as a critic), it becomes evident that it is impossible to impute to him a plagiarism that so flagrantly contradicts his own feelings on the matter of an author's rights in his own property.

I hope I shall not be thought cynical if I say that the strictures upon plagiarism quoted above are just such as I should have

[1] Edited by M. Plezia and St. Skimina, Wrocław, 1954.
[2] Wrocław–Kraków, Zakład Narodowy im. Ossolińskich, 1958.

expected to find in S.'s (or any contemporary) disquisitions on poetical composition, and that I see no psychological inconsistency between the expression of such theoretical opinions, or the personal diffidence of which W. gives examples, and the actual procedure adopted by S. He was faced with the problem of producing something that he felt was alien to his genius, and had ready to his hand something that seemed exactly to fit the case; 'After all', he may have said to himself, 'my rules forbidding plagiarism were never meant to apply to such a case as this. I shall have done no harm to anyone, and I shall not myself have committed any grievous sin, provided that I never actually publish the poems as my own'. The strict moralist might condemn him, but surely the psychologist would understand?